THE HAUNTED CONFEDERACY
GHOSTS OF THE CIVIL WAR SOUTH

Tales From
Alabama
Tennessee
Georgia &
Mississippi

Introduction – Echoes of a Haunted War

The American Civil War has been called many things: the nation's bloodiest conflict, a war between brothers, the crucible that reshaped the United States into something new and yet deeply scarred. It left more than six hundred thousand soldiers dead and untold thousands of civilians bereaved. Entire towns were burned, cities reduced to skeletal shells, and farmsteads shattered beyond repair. Yet the numbers, as overwhelming as they are, do not capture the full weight of the war's legacy. Behind each figure lies a life lost, a mother's grief, a widow's endless silence at the dinner table. Beyond the record books, beyond the grave markers and battlefield maps, there lingers something intangible — a residue of anguish, violence, and longing that clings to the places where men fought and families mourned.

To step onto Southern soil is to step onto a palimpsest: layers of life and death written over one another. In Tennessee, Alabama,

Mississippi, and Georgia, where the conflict raged at its hottest, the Civil War left not only scars on the land but also echoes in the air. Walk the old battlefields on a wind-swept night and you may feel history pressing close. The rustle of oak leaves can sound like a regiment advancing through underbrush; the hoot of an owl becomes the cry of the wounded; the thud of your own heartbeat echoes like distant drums. Imagination alone could explain such sensations, but the persistence of ghost stories — told for more than a century and a half, repeated by farmers, tourists, soldiers' descendants, and even skeptical historians — suggests that memory and haunting have fused into one.

Visitors still claim to hear phantom drums beating across the fields of Shiloh, steady as if a boy in uniform still keeps time for troops that never stop marching. In Franklin, Tennessee, the Lotz House, Carter House, and Carnton Plantation stand as a triangle of tragedy where thousands perished in a single evening, and where pale figures are said to pace the porches, eyes fixed on something beyond mortal sight. In Florence,

Alabama, the looming walls of Sweetwater Mansion shelter whispers and shadows, and in Pope's Tavern, the floorboards creak beneath unseen footsteps. Andersonville Prison in Georgia breathes sorrow from every ruined wall, and Chickamauga is haunted not only by soldiers but by the monstrous figure locals call Old Green Eyes, a presence as old as the land itself.

These are not simply tales spun for the delight of tourists in October, though ghost tours have indeed turned them into popular attractions. They are part of a cultural memory, woven into the identity of Southern towns and families. They emerge from trauma so profound that it could not be contained by the grave. Many of the mansions, taverns, and colleges we will visit in this book were raised during the hopeful antebellum years, their bricks laid by enslaved hands, their rooms decorated with dreams of prosperity. The war transformed them into hospitals, morgues, and strongholds. Blood soaked into their timbers, screams echoed through their corridors, and the grieving afterward left behind not just monuments but stories — stories that suggest some who suffered within those walls have never truly departed.

Shadows Cast by War

The Civil War was not confined to battlefields. It intruded into kitchens, parlors, nurseries, and churches. The front line often ran through a family's front yard. A woman could be baking bread in the morning and find her home commandeered by officers in the afternoon. A plantation's grand hall could host a ball one year and surgeries the next. The war blurred the boundaries between domestic life and carnage.

The scale of death staggered the imagination. At Shiloh alone, more than 23,000 were killed, wounded, or missing after two days of fighting. At Stones River, another 24,000 fell. At Gettysburg, the toll rose above 50,000. For families, the statistics translated into folded letters carried by neighbors: "He will not return." Often there was no body to bury. Men were interred in hastily dug trenches near where they fell, or in mass graves that held hundreds. In Franklin, bodies lay piled six deep in ditches, their faces already unrecognizable. In Vicksburg, soldiers were left where they collapsed during the siege, covered only when the smell became unbearable.

Such burials left the living with no closure. Bones surfaced decades later when rains washed away topsoil or when fields were plowed anew. Children stumbled upon skulls in the woods, and hunters found buttons and rusted buckles gleaming through leaves. Memory was not abstract. It was tactile, inescapable, sometimes literally underfoot.

In Tennessee and Alabama, where some of the fiercest fighting raged, the reminders were particularly vivid. Franklin, Murfreesboro, Decatur, and Florence all endured battles, occupations, or raids that left physical scars on their buildings. Bullet holes still pit the Carter House. The Old State Bank in Decatur stands as the only surviving bank building of its era in Alabama, its walls darkened by fire and its windows remembered as stages for a phantom widow's grief. In Florence, the cemetery's section called Soldier's Rest became a permanent gathering place for Confederate dead, their names lost, their whispers said to remain.

A Nation Turns to the Dead

Faced with such endless loss, Americans sought ways to reach beyond the veil. Out of that desperation, Spiritualism surged to prominence. The movement had begun in 1848 with the Fox Sisters of Hydesville, New York, whose supposed communication with spirits through knocks and rappings electrified audiences. By the 1850s, séances had spread across the country. They were sometimes parlor entertainments, sometimes sincere religious rituals. By the time war erupted, Spiritualism was firmly planted in both the North and South.

The unprecedented carnage gave Spiritualism new urgency. Families wanted to know: Where is he buried? Did he suffer? Does he forgive me for letting him go? A table that rapped once for "yes" and twice for "no" seemed to offer more comfort than silence. Mediums promised messages in faint voices, table-tippings, or the sudden cold rush of unseen hands.

Mary Todd Lincoln became Spiritualism's most famous adherent. After the death of her son Willie in 1862, she turned to mediums for solace. Séances were held in the White House itself. Witnesses describe a darkened room, a single candle flickering, and knocks echoing from the walls as Mrs. Lincoln asked her questions. Abraham Lincoln, skeptical yet curious, attended some of these sessions, his gaunt face half-lit in the gloom.

In the South, the devastation created its own Spiritualist circles. In towns like Franklin, Florence, and Decatur, grieving mothers and widows gathered in parlors. Imagine the flicker of oil lamps in Sweetwater Mansion, the heavy velvet curtains drawn, the hush as a medium placed her hands on a table. Outside, the night crickets chirped; inside, participants listened for faint taps. Was it the house settling, or the answer of a son lost at Chickamauga?

For those who sought solace, the line between haunting and Spiritualism blurred. The footsteps heard in Wesleyan Hall might be the ghost of a drummer boy or the manifestation conjured in a séance. The whispers in Pope's Tavern might be the groans of dying soldiers or the voices mediums claimed to call forth. The culture of Spiritualism gave vocabulary to experiences that otherwise defied explanation. It turned eerie noises into communication, shadows into presences, grief into contact.

Haunted Land, Haunted Houses

Each chapter of this book will explore a particular place where history and haunting intersect. Alabama and Tennessee provide the richest soil for these tales, but Georgia and Mississippi offer equally potent stories of anguish and spirits.

In Franklin, the Carter family huddled in their cellar while the battle raged overhead, cannonballs smashing into their home. Their son Tod was mortally wounded only yards from the house and brought inside to die. His footsteps are still said to echo through the rooms. Across the street, the Lotz House became a makeshift hospital, its floors slick with blood. Guests today whisper of drums beating faintly, of apparitions in period dress. And at Carnton Plantation, the bodies of four Confederate generals were laid out on the back porch under a blood-red moon. The porch remains a stage for spectral figures glimpsed in the corner of the eye.

In Florence, Sweetwater Mansion is a Gothic tableau. Built in 1835 by Robert Patton, it became a home, a hospital, and eventually a mausoleum of legend. Locals speak of a phantom coffin seen in the basement, of a boy named Billy whose laughter is sometimes heard in the halls. Paranormal investigators have recorded disembodied voices and doors slamming on their own. Some claim that séances were once held there, mediums asking the dead to reveal themselves — and that the house still responds.

Pope's Tavern, once a bustling inn, was transformed during the war into a place of amputation and agony. Soldiers' moans filled the rooms. Today, visitors report footsteps in empty corridors and the cries of the wounded echoing after dark. Wesleyan Hall, with its Gothic towers, was used by both Union and Confederate forces. Students and staff now tell stories of a drowned drummer boy whose beat still rattles through the hallways.

Florence City Cemetery holds a section called Soldier's Rest, where hundreds of Confederate dead were laid. Locals say that orbs float among the stones and that faint voices carry on the wind. Beside it lies the legend of Mountain Tom Clark, an outlaw lynched after the war, who boasted he would never be run over. He was buried beneath a street so wagons — and later cars — would prove him wrong. Some insist his spirit lingers by the cemetery wall, a restless echo of violence piled atop violence.

In Decatur, the Rhea–McEntire House and the Old State Bank stand as survivors of bombardment. They too are said to harbor spirits: generals still debating their plans, widows still weeping at windows. Across the South, from the prisons of Georgia to the siege lines of Mississippi, stories echo the same refrain: those who died in violence linger in unrest.

History Meets Haunting

This book does not set out to prove the existence of ghosts, nor to debunk them. It seeks to explore how history and haunting are entwined. Every ghost story is also a story of who lived and died, of how trauma shaped memory. To understand the apparitions said to walk the halls of Sweetwater or the fields of Shiloh, one must first understand what happened there — who built those places, who occupied them, who bled and wept within their walls.

The war ended in 1865, but the sorrow did not. Empty chairs at dinner tables became permanent. Graves marked "Unknown" multiplied across cemeteries. Children grew up never knowing their fathers. The living sought the dead in séances, in dreams, in stories told by firelight. And the dead, it seems, answered — in knocks, in whispers, in footsteps that never fade.

An Invitation

The chapters that follow will carry you through corridors where shadows whisper and across fields where silence is heavier than gunfire. You will encounter the phantom drummer of Stones River, the weeping soldier of Franklin, the ghost child of Sweetwater, the monstrous Old Green Eyes of Chickamauga, and countless nameless soldiers who still march in step across forgotten ground. Some stories arise from historical accounts, others from folklore, and still others from modern visitors who swear they felt a hand brush their arm when no one stood beside them.

This is not a collection of children's tales meant only to thrill. It is an exploration of how grief echoes through generations, how violence leaves its mark not only on monuments and archives but on air and shadow. To read these stories is to walk haunted ground.

Listen closely as the pages turn. The Civil War is not over. Its soldiers are still marching. Its wounded are still crying out. Its families are still calling across the veil.

And sometimes, if you are very quiet, they answer.

Chapter 1 – Shiloh: Phantom Drums in the Wilderness

On the banks of the Tennessee River, where the water curls silver through rolling woods and fields, lies a place that still trembles with echoes of war. Shiloh. The name itself means "place of peace," but in April 1862, it became the stage for one of the bloodiest clashes of the Civil War. More than 23,000 men were killed, wounded, or declared missing in just two days of fighting, a scale of carnage unprecedented at that time. Today, the fields and thickets where Confederate and Union soldiers once tore into each other with musket and bayonet are preserved as a national battlefield park, their open meadows and wooded hollows serene beneath the sky. Yet beneath that calm, locals and visitors alike speak of something unsettled.

Shiloh is not only remembered in textbooks and monuments; it is remembered in whispers of phantom drums, spectral troops seen marching at twilight, cries of the wounded carried on the wind, and an atmosphere that chills even on the warmest spring morning. For those who walk the land at dusk, when the light fades through the trees and mist clings to the ground, Shiloh feels like a battlefield not entirely past.

The Battle Before the Haunting

To understand the hauntings of Shiloh, one must first understand the ferocity of the battle itself. The fight began at dawn on April 6, 1862, when Confederate General Albert Sidney Johnston launched a surprise assault against Union General Ulysses S. Grant's army encamped near Pittsburg Landing. For months, Union troops had been gathering along the Tennessee River in preparation for an advance into the heart of the Confederacy. Johnston sought to strike before reinforcements could arrive.

The Confederate attack shattered the morning stillness. Gunfire rolled through the woods, and Union soldiers, many of them raw recruits, stumbled awake to find themselves under siege. They scrambled from tents as musket balls tore through canvas, the woods filling with the acrid smoke of black powder. Confederates pushed forward with bayonets flashing, and the Union lines reeled backward toward the river.

Among the farm clearings and woodlots, the fighting turned savage. Men grappled hand to hand, clubbing with musket stocks, stabbing with bayonets. The ground became slippery with blood. Families living in the area fled or hid in cellars, listening to the roar of cannon as their fields became killing grounds. By afternoon, General Johnston himself was struck by a bullet and bled to death in the thickets near a peach orchard in full blossom. Witnesses said the petals fell like snow, drifting over his lifeless body as if nature mourned.

Grant's army, though battered, held the line. Through the night, Union reinforcements arrived, ferried across the Tennessee River. On April 7, the Union counterattacked. By evening, the Confederates were forced into retreat, leaving the field to the Federals. The toll was staggering: 13,000 Union casualties, 10,600 Confederate. The battle stunned both North and South, shattering illusions that the war would be short or bloodless.

The Dead and the Land

The battlefield, littered with the dead and dying, became a charnel ground. Corpses lay thick across the peach orchard, by the Sunken Road, and in the dense undergrowth of the Hornet's Nest, where Union troops had made a desperate stand. Many bodies were hastily buried in shallow graves; others were left exposed for days. Rainstorms unearthed corpses, and scavenging animals prowled the field. The stench carried for miles.

Local civilians were conscripted to bury the dead, often in mass trenches. Survivors wrote of men tossing bodies into pits by the wagonload, faces already unrecognizable, uniforms soaked in blood. Soldiers who returned to the site months later described bones protruding from the soil, skulls scattered in ravines. Farmers complained for years afterward of plowing up fragments of belts, buttons, and bone. Shiloh was not just a memory — it was a wound still open, bleeding into the land itself.

For the men who survived, Shiloh became a nightmare that haunted their dreams. Letters home spoke of the unending screams of the wounded, of comrades cut down in front of them. Some veterans swore they could still hear the battle when they closed their eyes. Such impressions seeped into the collective imagination. If men felt haunted in their minds, it was only a short step to the belief that the ground itself was haunted too.

Phantom Drums and Ghostly Regiments

The most persistent legend of Shiloh is the sound of phantom drums. Visitors walking the battlefield at dusk or dawn have reported hearing the steady cadence of a drumline, as if unseen soldiers were marching in formation through the mist. The drumming often fades when one approaches, only to start again farther off, leading witnesses deeper into the woods. Rangers and guides, though cautious about endorsing ghost stories, admit that enough people report the same experience to make it a fixture of Shiloh lore.

Some say the drumming comes from the spirit of a young Confederate drummer boy who fell in the first hours of battle. Accounts tell of his body found beside a shattered drum, its skin split and spattered with blood. His duty had been to beat time, to keep soldiers moving in rhythm, and so in death he keeps the cadence still. Others believe the drumming is residual — the sound of whole regiments imprinted on the land, endlessly marching toward a fate already sealed.

Along with the drums, visitors report ghostly soldiers. Pale figures in butternut or blue have been seen moving among the trees, faces obscured, their forms dissolving into mist when approached. At the Hornet's Nest, where Union troops endured repeated charges, some witnesses claim to have seen spectral lines of men rising from the ground itself, muskets at the ready, only to vanish when the wind shifts. One woman visiting with her children swore she saw a soldier in ragged gray limping through the field, his uniform torn, his face waxy and pale. When she called out, he turned to her, eyes blank as glass, and disappeared.

Night amplifies the unease. Campers who stay in the area tell of footsteps pacing outside their tents, of muffled cries and groans, of the unmistakable metallic clatter of bayonets. Some wake to find their lanterns extinguished, though no wind stirred. On more than one occasion, visitors claim to have felt a sudden, icy hand brush their shoulder, though the night was warm and still.

The Crying Angels of Shiloh Church

The battle takes its name from a small log church that stood near the center of the fighting — Shiloh Church. During the battle, the church was shelled, riddled with bullets, and splintered by cannon fire. Afterward, it served as a field hospital, its floors slick with blood, pews used as makeshift cots. Surgeons worked by lantern light, the screams of the wounded echoing against the wooden walls. Amputated limbs were piled outside, the air rank with blood and disinfectant.

Today, a replica of the church stands on the battlefield, but locals insist that something of the original remains in spirit. On quiet nights, people claim to hear the low moans of men in agony drifting from its walls, even when the building is empty. Some visitors have reported faint hymns sung by ghostly voices, as if the congregation still gathers. There are also stories of "crying angels": indistinct figures seen kneeling in the grass nearby, weeping into their hands. Whether they are spirits of nurses, wives, or simply the collective grief of the place given form, they remind visitors that Shiloh was never truly a place of peace.

Lights in the Wilderness

Another common phenomenon at Shiloh is the appearance of strange lights. Battlefield guides have noted flickering orbs glowing in the woods, especially near the Sunken Road. Sometimes they appear red, like lanterns carried through the mist; other times they are blue-white, darting between trees. Skeptics dismiss them as swamp gas or reflections, but many visitors remain unconvinced.

One veteran of the First World War, visiting Shiloh in the 1920s, wrote in his diary that he saw "lanterns bobbing among the thickets" where no paths existed. He approached, believing rangers were patrolling, but the lights vanished at once. He later told his family that he had seen the ghosts of soldiers carrying their lanterns, still searching for the wounded they could not save.

Even today, tourists armed with cameras hope to capture the lights. Paranormal investigators claim to have photographed orbs hovering in places where thousands died. Whether tricks of the lens or echoes of the past, the lights have become part of the legend of Shiloh — spectral beacons in the wilderness.

Spiritualism and the Battlefield

The rise of Spiritualism during and after the Civil War intersects with Shiloh's legacy. Families who lost sons there often turned to mediums, seeking answers about their fate. In nearby towns, séances were held in darkened parlors, participants asking spirits to rap once for yes, twice for no. Shiloh, with its staggering death toll and its shallow graves, loomed large in such gatherings.

Some stories tell of mothers who traveled to the battlefield itself, kneeling by mass graves and whispering their son's name, hoping to hear a reply. Spiritualist newspapers of the era printed letters describing "unquiet places" where the veil between the living and dead was thin. Shiloh was frequently mentioned, its very name — "peace" — sounding ironic against the restless reports of the haunted.

Modern paranormal groups sometimes frame Shiloh as one of the strongest examples of "residual haunting," where traumatic energy imprints itself on the land. The phantom drums, the spectral regiments, the cries in the night — all of these, they argue, are replays of the past, bound to the ground by sheer force of anguish. But others insist that the spirits are active, aware, sometimes even reaching out to the living.

Modern Shiloh

Today, Shiloh National Military Park preserves the battlefield with monuments, reconstructed trenches, and markers detailing the events of April 1862. Visitors walk manicured paths, read plaques, and hear the official history. Yet for many, the atmosphere itself is the truest guide. Rangers acknowledge that countless guests have reported eerie sensations. Some scoff, others lean in and whisper their own accounts of cold spots, strange noises, and shadowy figures glimpsed out of the corner of the eye.

At night, when the park is closed and the woods stand silent, locals say the battlefield belongs to the dead. The river murmurs nearby, the trees sigh in the wind, and the ground seems to breathe. If you listen carefully, you may hear the steady beat of a drum. If you look too long at the mist, you may see men marching, their faces pale, their eyes empty, their steps taking them nowhere but deeper into eternity.

Shiloh is remembered in monuments and books, but it is also remembered in whispers and shadows. Its story is one of blood and anguish, of courage and horror, of the human toll of war. And in the silence that follows gunfire, in the mist that follows dawn, the dead still linger. The drummer keeps his cadence. The soldiers keep their march. The battlefield itself keeps its ghosts.

Chapter 2 – Chickamauga: Old Green Eyes and the Phantom Armies

The Cherokee had long spoken of this valley as a place of foreboding. They called the waters Tsikama'gi — the "River of Death." Settlers repeated the name without understanding, using it to mark the gentle creek that wound through cedar woods and farmland near the Tennessee–Georgia line. But when September 1863 came, the name no longer felt poetic or strange. It felt inevitable. In two days, more than 34,000 men were killed, wounded, or declared missing in the Battle of Chickamauga. The land became a slaughterhouse, the air itself thick with smoke and cries. The River of Death lived up to its name, and it drank deep.

From that moment forward, Chickamauga was remembered not only in strategy books or casualty rolls but in whispers, in shadows, in sightings that defied reason. Phantom regiments still march at dusk. Horses scream in the night. And always there is the creature with burning green eyes, watching from the trees — the sentinel of Chickamauga, as old as legend and as restless as the dead themselves.

A Land of Memory Before the Guns

Before the armies came, Chickamauga was farmland. Scotch-Irish families raised cabins of hewn logs, fields of corn, and small orchards. Enslaved African Americans bent over the rows, built fences, and carried the weight of the households. The Lafayette Road, cutting through the heart of the valley, linked farms and markets with Chattanooga to the north.

But woven through that daily life were stories older than the cabins. The Cherokee had once hunted these ridges and claimed that spirits walked here. Strange cries echoed in the woods, they said, and green lights burned at night. Some spoke of a guardian creature with luminous eyes that glared from the underbrush. Settlers passed on the tales, calling the place uncanny. By the time war came, the legends had already soaked into the soil.

The Clash of Armies

The Union Army of the Cumberland under Major General William Rosecrans pushed south from Tennessee in late 1863, threatening Confederate control of the region. General Braxton Bragg, desperate to halt them, chose ground along Chickamauga Creek to make his stand.

On September 19, the armies collided in the woods. The cedar brakes were so dense that men stumbled blindly, muskets firing at flashes of shadow. Whole brigades disappeared into smoke and did not return. Union regiments found themselves flanked and surrounded; Confederates stumbled into crossfire and fell in heaps. Soldiers described the fighting as "blind, close, terrible."

The next day, Confederate General James Longstreet exploited a gap in the Union line. His men poured through, shattering Rosecrans's right flank. Panic spread, and Rosecrans himself galloped off the field, convinced all was lost. Yet on Snodgrass Hill, Union General George H. Thomas held his ground with stubborn resolve. His troops repelled wave after wave until night fell. For that stand he earned the title "The Rock of Chickamauga," though thousands of his men lay broken around him.

When the guns fell silent, the ground was thick with the dead. Men lay piled in ravines, tangled in brambles, slumped against shattered trees. Horses screamed until they were shot to end their misery. Civilians crept back to homes only to find fences flattened and orchards filled with corpses. One farmer's daughter later said: "The earth looked as if it had grown bodies in place of corn."

Aftermath and Burial

The aftermath of Chickamauga lingered for weeks. The stench of decay clung to the valley. Burial details worked frantically, but the scale was overwhelming. Many bodies were interred in shallow trenches or covered hastily with brush and dirt. Others were left where they fell until rain or animals scattered their bones. Travelers in the years that followed wrote of stumbling upon skulls in the undergrowth, or of plowing up bones when fields were cleared. The land was never entirely at rest.

Families came searching for loved ones, combing the battlefield for trinkets or uniforms that might prove identity. Few succeeded. The unknown dead far outnumbered the named. Such incompleteness fed the stories that would grow in the decades after — stories of men who could not leave because no one had marked their graves.

Phantom Regiments

The most common reports from Chickamauga are of soldiers who never stopped marching. At dusk, when the mist curls low and the trees blur into shadow, visitors hear the tramp of feet on gravel. Sometimes there is the faint roll of drums, sometimes the metallic clink of muskets shifting. Then the forms appear: pale, half-seen, moving in formation across open fields. They march toward the tree line and dissolve into nothing.

Hunters camping near the Lafayette Road in the early 1900s swore they awoke to the clash of muskets and the cries of charging men. Sparks of light flickered in the fog, bayonets gleamed, and then the entire scene dissolved. Park rangers in the twentieth century have quietly admitted that tourists frequently approach them shaken, insisting they saw a column of soldiers where no reenactment was taking place. The impression is always the same: the battle continues.

Some accounts speak not of marching but of fighting. Visitors have reported hearing gunfire crack from nowhere, or voices shouting "Forward!" only to be swallowed by silence. One man in the 1930s claimed he saw two spectral figures locked in combat, bayonets fixed, their faces pale and indistinct, before both melted into the mist.

Old Green Eyes

More terrifying than phantom troops is the figure known as Old Green Eyes. His legend predates the battle, but the bloodshed seems to have bound him permanently to the land.

Descriptions vary wildly. Some insist he is the ghost of a Confederate soldier decapitated by cannon fire, his body searching eternally for its missing head. His eyes, glowing green, are said to wander independently through the night, peering from bushes or floating across fields. Others claim he is older still — a Cherokee spirit, a guardian of the valley who feeds on carnage. Still others say he is a beast, crouching low, his hair long and tangled, his teeth bared, his glowing eyes fixed on the living.

Farmers in the late nineteenth century spoke of being followed by two green lights as they walked home from fields. Couples driving the park roads in the twentieth century reported eyes rising suddenly from the ground, floating toward them, forcing them to flee in terror. Rangers on night patrols have had horses panic and bolt, their riders convinced that something unseen watched from the ridges. Paranormal investigators in recent decades treat Old Green Eyes as the centerpiece of Chickamauga lore, setting cameras and recorders in the cedar woods. Some return with photographs of luminous orbs. Others record guttural growls too deep for human throats.

Old Green Eyes is not merely a ghost. He is a legend fused with the land, a shape that belongs as much to memory as to terror. Chickamauga is his domain, and those who enter after dark do so under his gaze.

Spirits of the Horses

Chickamauga's ghosts are not only human. Horses, whose screams filled the air during the battle, are said to haunt the fields. Visitors have reported hearing the thunder of hooves across open ground, though no riders appear. Others tell of a massive black stallion charging through the mist, mane streaming, only to vanish into thin air.

A park employee once described hearing frantic hooves circling him near dusk. The ground trembled, the noise rose to a frenzy — and then silence. He stood alone in the clearing, heart pounding, certain he had just been surrounded by ghostly cavalry.

The Snodgrass House

The Snodgrass farm became the final bastion of Union defense. For two days, George H. Thomas held the hill there against repeated Confederate charges. Inside the Snodgrass House, the wounded poured in until the floors were slick with blood. Surgeons sawed through bone in endless shifts, tossing limbs into piles outside the door. The family cowered in the cellar, listening to the screams above.

Today, the house is preserved as part of the park. Visitors often describe sudden drops in temperature, shadows that cross the hall, or the sound of boots pacing upstairs. Some have heard moans and prayers in the night. A ranger once claimed he glimpsed a lantern moving from room to room when the building was locked and empty. The Snodgrass House, more than a century later, still carries its burden.

Spiritualism and Memory

Chickamauga fed not only the ground but the imagination. In the years after the war, Spiritualism surged. Families sought mediums to reach sons lost at Chickamauga, asking: Where is he buried? Did he suffer? Does he forgive me? Séances in parlors across Tennessee invoked the name of the River of Death as if it were a gate to the other side.

One Spiritualist paper in the 1870s printed a supposed message from a "soldier of Chickamauga": "We fell like wheat, and we rise like mist. Tell my mother I stand in the cedars and I am not alone." Whether fraud or faith, such words only deepened the conviction that the battlefield was alive with spirits.

The River of Death

Today, Chickamauga and Chattanooga National Military Park preserves those ridges and fields. Monuments dot the land; plaques recount movements and casualties. Yet history is not confined to markers. At dusk the cedars close in, the mist thickens, and silence falls heavy. Visitors often feel watched. Some hear the tramp of feet in gravel. Others glimpse pale figures vanishing into the trees. And always there is the possibility of green eyes glowing in the dark.

The Cherokee named it the River of Death long before 1863. The Civil War only confirmed it. Chickamauga is not merely history. It is a mausoleum without walls, a place where the dead march still, where the monster still prowls, and where the land itself refuses to forget.

Chapter 3 – Franklin: Houses of the

Haunted Line

When the last light of November slipped behind the low hills, Franklin was still a town of porches and parlors, of cotton rows and orchard windbreaks and the hushed clatter of kitchen work ending for the day. The Harpeth River turned like dull steel in the gloaming. Stoves were banked, lamps trimmed. In the parlor of a well-made brick house on Columbia Pike, a grandfather clock tolled the hour with the soft patience of a long-settled life. And then the hour shattered.

The first volleys sounded like doors slamming across the valley, then like ten thousand doors, then like thunder that had learned to roar in a human tongue. The Union works ran like a ridge across the southern edge of town, a rough wall of dirt and rails thrown up in an anxious afternoon. From the south, John Bell Hood's Army of Tennessee surged through the cold, gray dusk—men who had marched hungry and angry for days, men whose boots were already split, who could smell Nashville on the air. Officers waved their swords and shouted the word that has always divided the living from the dead: forward. And Franklin, peaceful that morning, became a furnace.

They called it five hours of fire. The Union line flamed in a sheet, the Confederates broke against it like surf. A cotton gin near the Carter farm became a landmark that was less a building than a silhouette—muscled with men in blue, wreathed in smoke. The first Confederate wave struck and slid, the second jammed into the first, the third climbed over the bodies of the first two. Bullets clipped fence pickets into white dust; rails leapt apart; boards flew into the night like birds. The air tasted of powder and iron and the faint sweetness of crushed apples from a nearby orchard ground underfoot. By midnight, the lanes were stacked with the fallen, and stick-fences were webbed with torn cloth and hair. Franklin did not see a battle so much as wear one.

It would never take that garment off again.

The Carter House

Fountain Branch Carter built his house in 1830, a neat Federal rectangle of brick and balance, a craftsman's statement that he intended to stand and be counted in the little town just off the Nashville road. The main block faced Columbia Pike with a clear-eyed symmetry; behind it, outbuildings and a cotton gin served the farm's daily work. His son Tod grew into a quick, laughing young man with a touch of show about him, useful in business and charming at a gathering. He left to join the Confederate army and carried the family's pride with him. The house remained full—daughters, grandchildren, enslaved people at work in the yard, neighbors coming and going through the front hall that smelled of beeswax and turpentine.

On November 30th the Union army took the Carter place as an anchor, and men in blue dug their trenches into the family's fields. The Carters were told, in the practiced calm of officers who have said such things on other doorsteps, to go below. They crowded into the basement: Fountain Branch, his wife, the daughters and their children, a tangle of skirts and jackets, a quilt thrown over a trembling pair of knees. They listened as the world upstairs turned to hammers and yelling, the floor trembling as if an enormous animal had begun to breathe right there under the joists. Someone tried to pray and the words came out like stones.

The cotton gin out in the yard—its angles like a child's drawing of a house—was hammered to a dark mass by the fire that swept around it. In the swirl of combat a figure broke free, staggered near the Carter lane, and was surrounded by men in gray who shouted his name. Tod. Their brother, their son, cut down almost home. They carried him in with a daredevil tenderness, men who had just crawled through a storm gentling their hands to lift a single wounded body past the bullet-bruised doorframe. They laid him in an upstairs room where he had read by lamplight as a boy. A sister held a candle, and the flame trembled a little in the draft that sneaked through the shattered sash. Someone said his name again, a mother-syllable, flat with disbelief. Tod Carter opened his eyes once and then closed them, and the house swallowed that last breath like a confession.

The Carter House did not empty when the troops moved on. It filled again, this time with the wounded. Doors came off their hinges to become tables. Mattresses were dragged from beds, bedcovers shredded into bandages. The parlor smelled of powder and laudanum and blood so sweet it turned the stomach. Someone—there is always someone—found a pencil and scrawled a name and regiment on a scrap of wood and set it beside a still hand, as if the wood might tell a wife later what the mouth could not.

Today the Carter House still wears its scars openly. You can count the bullet marks on the walls. Your fingers dip into them without your permission, as if the hand wants to learn what the eyes already know. But there are marks you cannot touch. Guides will tell you that footsteps pace upstairs long after closing, that a soft male voice—never loud, always close—says a single name in a room where a candle once trembled. They will tell you about the evening a volunteer locked up, turned to cross the yard, and saw a young man in light trousers and a short shell jacket walking fast near the fence line, his head cocked like a boy listening for his father's call. She shouted, thinking him a straggler. He vanished before he reached the road. On heavy summer nights the air in the basement grows close, and visitors complain not of heat but pressure, the weight of many people pressed together in the dark, trying not to breathe too loudly. The house remains a ledger: blood in one column, footsteps in the other, the sum never quite balancing.

The Lotz House

Across the pike stands proof that the antebellum South could carve beauty with its own hands. Johann Albert Lotz came from Germany with a carpenter's eye and a head full of fretwork. In 1858 he raised his house as both shelter and showroom: mantels cut like lace, newel posts with dignity, a parlor made to show what wood can do when it is loved. His wife, Margaretha, kept the rooms bright; children ran up and down stairs designed to be walked on in admiration. The house looked across to the Carters' with neighborly confidence. Franklin was a small place; its houses were like kin who had chosen different clothes.

Lotz knew wood and knew what fire did to it. When the lines formed in the afternoon and guns began to bark, he took his family by the shoulders and drove them across the road to the brick basement he believed would hold. He had carved the banister himself, and he did not look back at it; it is a gift to a house when its maker denies himself a last look before a storm. They were in the Carter cellar when the storm broke.

In the morning he brought them home. The Lotz House had been chewed by cannon and musket and boots. The floors—they were not floors now but books recording the same word on every page. In the weeks that followed, his poor house learned to be a hospital. The clever mantels witnessed surgeries and did not crack under the weight of seeing. The banister was gripped by so many hands—some shaking, some gone white—that its sheen changed. In the yard, arms and legs joined the piles of cast-off rails, and the road's traffic was a procession of pain.

People say houses listen long after we stop speaking to them. The Lotz House appears to have learned the habit too well. Visitors hear a drum. It is not bold; it is the drum a boy would beat in a parlor so his father might be proud. It sounds once, twice, a short roll, then stillness. If you stand in the front room late and close your eyes, the plaster carries a rhythm you feel in your collarbone.

The colder stories are colder because they come dressed as ordinary moments. A staff member climbs the stairs, thinking about a clipboard, and sees a woman's hem vanish around a landing—no rush, no flourish—only the steady glide of someone used to carrying water and cloth. The staff member calls out, and no one answers. In the morning the interior doors are found drawn to within a hand's width of the jambs, every one, as if someone moved through the rooms in the night and could not bear them to be fully open. In the dining room a visitor catches the smell of hot iron and tallow and realizes it is not a candle at all but a lamp burned for work—late work, hard work, the kind a carpenter does when the house itself needs mending. Once, in the late afternoon, a guide heard a phrase in German as clear as the thump of a book on a table. She turned, but only the carved mantel was looking back at her, its garlands patient, its edges soft with age. There is a tenderness in this haunting, a craftsman's love poured into pine and poplar that refuses to leave when the bleeding is done.

Carnton

South beyond town, on a rise where the breeze can find a porch even on the hottest August day, stands Carnton. Randal McGavock began it in 1826, built it to host, to preside, to look down a long drive with a calm that only inherited confidence can teach. By the 1860s John and Carrie McGavock kept the house, its rooms squared with habit and duty. Enslaved men and women worked the fields and kitchens and carried the weight while the family received and entertained. The back gallery was the sort of stage Southern houses fashion for themselves—somewhere between a throne and a neighbor's stoop. On November 30th it became an altar.

When the lines broke and the screaming began to sound like a single river choked with stones, the wounded came to Carnton. They did not ask; they came like weather. The house did not refuse them. Surgeons set up in the rooms upstairs, in the big bedrooms meant for sleep and gossip and babies. They laid men down on carpets that had been bought with the confidence of a good harvest. They worked by lamplight, by lanterns, by whatever could be made to hold flame. The floorboards learned the weight of blood, its smell and slick, and the sound steel makes when it bites bone and is withdrawn, and the guilty relief a man feels when the screaming he hears is not his own.

On the gallery, four generals lay in a row. Patrick Cleburne, Hiram Granbury, John Adams, States Rights Gist—names that already had a certain ringing to them, now spoken in the flat tone reserved for the dead. A lantern swung once and steadied. The faces were younger than stories would later make them, the hands familiar with writing orders and adjusting gloves, now still. In the half-light there is always movement where there is none: flame makes death a little beautiful for a second. Dawn takes that gift away.

In the days that followed, Carnton did what houses do when families insist on being more than proprietors. Carrie McGavock cut bandages and moved through rooms with the thoughtless grace of women who have made four hundred dinners and will make four hundred more even if the world collapses. She stood on the porch and let men who could not stand stand on her arm. The field beyond the house filled with graves. Years later the McGavocks oversaw the careful exhumation of scattered dead and the creation of a cemetery that looks, from a distance, like an orchard of white fruit.

Carnton is not a building so much as a body with memories in its joints. Visitors tell of footsteps that cross upstairs when there is no one to cross them. Doors close—not slammed, but with the firmness of someone carrying a tray into a room where men are trying to sleep. Some see a woman in black on the back gallery, a shadow that knows where to step without looking, that pauses at the top of the stairs as if listening for the breath of a thousand men. I cannot prove it is Carrie; I cannot prove it is not. What I can tell you is this: people cry on that porch without knowing why, and no one thinks less of them for it.

As for the stains on the floors—if you are the sort of reader who prefers prosaic explanations, you will say that wood remembers liquids as color and that time pulls the color up sometimes like a bruise returning after it has gone. If you are the sort who believes in an account kept in more than dollars and cents, you will stand very still in the upper rooms and let your eyes adjust. Either way, there are places in Carnton where the boards seem to darken from within, as if a low tide has revealed a line it cannot cross.

The Weeping Soldier

He appears most often where the wind moves a little, near the edge of the McGavock Confederate Cemetery, where the rows are straight in the way only grief insists upon. He does not always wear the same coat. Sometimes it is a shell jacket the color of wet bark with buttons like moons; sometimes it is blue, Union issue, sleeves too long, as if the quartermaster measured him wrong and promised him time to grow. Sometimes the cloth hangs in ribbons. But his posture is always the same: a man trying to breathe through the weight on his chest.

He is not theatrical. He does not summon a storm or lift his face to scream. He stands with his head bowed and the round of his cap brim is the only sharp line left, and his shoulders shake in a way that makes a watching stranger feel impolite. If you call out, he startles—not up, not toward, but away, the way a deer startles, into the trees or a fold of ground or into nothing at all as if the field has learned how to accept a body after all these years of failing at it.

Children see him more often than adults. They pull at their mother's sleeve and say the crying man lost his hat, or that the crying man is looking for a dog, or they simply point and then insist, later at dinner, that they were not pointing at "just air." A groundskeeper mending a fence heard a wet sound once—the sound of a man catching his breath wrong—and turned to find no one, only the rank of white markers and the little flags very gently quivering as if a great coat had brushed past. Tourists walk out with packages from a bookstore tucked under the arm, intent on finding inscription dates, and come back pale and embarrassed because they did not expect to feel anything and now cannot politely stop.

What does he weep for? A single friend, perhaps, whose pocket held the letter home that said we are winning, we are fine. Or a son. Or a brother. Or the fact that he himself cannot seem to find his own place to lie down. Some decide he is an emblem, a grief gathered from a thousand mouths and worn as a single mask. But the simplest answer is often truest: the Weeping Soldier weeps because the ground still asks him to.

The Long Night and the Long After

The battle took its breath in five hours and exhaled slowly for years. Franklin learned how to be quiet in a way that is not peace. After the armies moved toward Nashville, townspeople returned to their porches with pails and rakes and sheets. They moved quietly not for reverence but because noise collapses under the weight of a task like that. Wagons creaked with bodies and with things that had been part of bodies. Men walked with a carefully practiced lack of attention to faces. Women brought water and did not put the pitchers down until the handles burned the palms. Children were sent to carry notes to neighbors because the grown were too busy or too broken to trust themselves to knock and speak.

In houses, the work was the same in a different shape. Floors were scrubbed until the nails showed new. Basins were emptied and scoured and filled again. Windows were opened to throw the smell of chloroform and sweat and fear into air that did not want it. Churchyards filled. A new math governed speech—less mother-of-three, more widow-of-one. The Carters stood in a house that had done what it could and then had to keep standing. At Carnton, the porch kept its vigil not for hours but for generations.

The mind's ear remembers what the mind's eye cannot bear. People who have never believed in ghosts find, years later, that they cannot stand in the Carter yard at dusk without hearing a sound like leather on gravel, or the brief clicking of a buckle against a musket band, a sound so small it seems ridiculous to notice until you realize there is no buckle and no musket and your throat is tight anyway. In the Lotz parlor the afternoon sun throws a windowpane onto the floor in a fat square of gold and the dust inside it swirls differently, like men moving and stopping and moving again. On the Carnton gallery a visitor rests his hand on the rail and takes it away quickly because, just for a moment, the wood felt warmer than the air as if someone else's palm had been there a second before.

Franklin has its stories of night work too. The woman who keeps a key and walks the empty house one last time hears a low voice say "water" from a stair half-landing where no mouth waits. The man on a late tour lingers on the porch to finish a question and sees, not with his eyes but with the old animal sense that once kept us from falling off cliffs at dusk, that he is not alone at the gallery's far end. When he looks, there is nothing. His heart thunders anyway. On a winter evening with the high whine of wind through bare limbs, a volunteer locking the cemetery gate hears a single bootstep in leaves and thinks ah, a stray visitor—and turns to see only a row of stones with all their brief stories chiseled thinner and thinner by the weather.

Spiritualism in a Town of Two Midnights

When the war ended for other places, Franklin still had two midnights—one on the clock and one in the mind. In the late 1860s and 1870s the South learned the parlor trick of calling the dead by name. Séances took their place between supper and sleep. In Franklin they sometimes began with a prayer and a stubbornness of chin, because even those who doubted wanted to try once, only once, to ask where the body lay, whether it hurt, whether forgiveness was possible. In houses not far from the Carter place, a medium sat with fingertips on a table's edge and listened for taps; in a room near the Lotz stair a tight circle held hands until the heat of palms made the air stuffy; in a side parlor at Carnton, a widow in black leaned forward and whispered a name she had not spoken aloud in daylight for months.

Whether the knocks were tricks or grief given a voice does not matter much to a town with two midnights. What matters is that the asking never quite stopped. Every ghost story is also a prayer with its grammar bent by need. The people of Franklin learned to ask differently—less show, more ache. The answers, when they came, came the way answers often do: in the form of a sudden smell of lamp oil, or a voice that sounds like a remembered voice but says a new word, or a draft that moves against the closed window as if a man had walked past and left the air to pick up his pace.

The Battlefield That Does Not Empty

Walk the pike south of town in late light and the fields look simple again—lines of dark soil, stubble the color of old pennies, the Harpeth sliding cold and self-possessed toward its next bend. Then something shifts. The air thickens the way water does when you step from the shallows toward the deep. Fence posts that seemed random take on the geometry of formations. A stand of cedars suddenly looks like a place men would choose to run to or from. Your eyes pick out a low swell and call it a breastwork though the earth shows nothing but its winter fur.

You might hear it first: that small, practical sound of equipment moving with the body that owns it—metal on leather, leather on cloth, cloth on bone. Then you might see only shadow, and then you might see men. They will not be in the clean lines of parades; they will be in the tense arrangement of men who are afraid and moving anyway. They will go where the old line was and disappear into air they wore out a long time ago. If you are unlucky, you will try to follow with your eyes; if you are lucky, you will let them go where they have been going for a hundred and sixty years and look at the ground instead, because what needs looking at is not always what shines.

The houses stand that night as they stood that other night: the Carter House square and stubborn, the Lotz House with its carved restraint, Carnton lifted to catch the breeze that carries the cemetery's breath. Each holds to its work. One keeps the name of a son in a single room where a candle fought a draft. One holds the rhythm a boy beat to be brave. One walks the porch with a woman in black who will not set the tray down until the last man is sleeping. And in the ranks beyond the gate, a soldier weeps without shame.

Franklin is not a moral—it will not make you better. It is not a sermon—it has nothing to explain. It is a place where wood and brick and earth have learned to remember. If you stand still long enough, they will lend that memory to you for the space of a breath. And if you find yourself weeping on a porch where you meant only to listen, or whispering a name in a cemetery where you meant only to read, take it like communion and leave lightly. The living are guests here. The hosts are busy.

Chapter 4 – Alabama's Haunted Ground

Alabama is a state stitched together by red clay, pine thickets, and limestone ridges. Beneath its hills and valleys runs a hidden underworld: a network of caves, caverns, and darkened passages carved by water into the bones of the land. In Lauderdale, Colbert, and Limestone Counties, this karst terrain yawns open in sinkholes and cave mouths, and locals have long whispered that the ground itself is unstable not only in a geological sense but in a spiritual one. Paranormal researchers often note that limestone is a common denominator in haunted places, part of the so-called "stone tape theory," which suggests that stone can trap the energy of human suffering and replay it like a record. If there is any truth to that, then northern Alabama is a kind of vast phonograph of the dead, its caves and chambers storing the anguish of war.

Here, the Civil War left its scar on the landscape, and with it came the hauntings that still echo through Florence, Tuscumbia, and Decatur. Mansions that once gleamed with antebellum pride became hospitals. Taverns turned into headquarters. College halls were seized for barracks. And the cemeteries filled until new sections were cut into the earth. To this day, these places breathe uneasily.

In Florence especially, the ghosts seem tied to both blood and stone. The city sits on the southern bank of the Tennessee River, a crossing point coveted by Union and Confederate alike. The river valley rests atop layers of Mississippian limestone, riddled with caves like Dust Cave and Red Bone Cave. Locals mutter that the underground and the above ground bleed into one another here, that the echoes of musketry still reverberate off hidden walls below. When the wind is just right, they say, the earth itself seems to moan.

Sweetwater Mansion

Sweetwater Mansion sits on the edge of Florence, a white-columned antebellum home built in 1835 by General John Brahan, a War of 1812 veteran and one of the city's founding figures. The home later passed to Robert Patton, who would become Alabama's governor during Reconstruction. Its broad portico, tall windows, and elegant interior made it a symbol of Southern wealth. Yet from the start, the mansion carried shadows. Slaves worked its grounds, and tragedies threaded through its family line. By the time the Civil War arrived, Sweetwater was already marked by sorrow.

The war made it worse. Confederate officers are said to have used the home, its parlors filled with anxious maps and the clatter of boots. Wounded soldiers were brought to its rooms. Some claim one of the Patton sons died in the house during the war, his coffin resting in an upstairs room until burial. In later years, visitors swore they saw the coffin itself reappear — a spectral casket materializing in the corner, its lid slightly ajar, the air in the room turning icy as if the death were happening all over again.

Sweetwater is notorious for its hauntings. Guides and guests report apparitions of a soldier pacing the upstairs hallway, his boots echoing on the old pine. Women in long dresses glide through the parlors, their faces obscured. Some visitors have been shoved or scratched by unseen hands. Cold spots flare in corners; doors slam shut with violent force. Paranormal investigators note that Sweetwater sits atop rich limestone bedrock — a natural reservoir for the energies of trauma. They speculate that the very walls are "charged" by what the house has seen.

At night the house looms against the dark, its windows catching moonlight like eyes. More than one caretaker has refused to stay alone after hearing footsteps cross the second floor when the building was locked and empty. Sweetwater Mansion is not just a relic of Florence's antebellum pride; it is a vessel for its ghosts.

Pope's Tavern

In the heart of Florence stands Pope's Tavern, a brick inn and stagecoach stop dating to the early 1800s. Before the war it welcomed travelers, its rooms echoing with the laughter of merchants and the clink of glasses. But by 1861, it had become something darker. Both Union and Confederate forces used the tavern as a hospital. The building that once rang with song was drowned in groans.

Surgeons worked on its tables, blades flashing in lamplight, sawdust scattered across the floors to soak the blood. Amputated limbs were tossed out the windows into piles that grew until they were carted away. The tavern's walls absorbed the cries of men begging for water, for morphine, for their mothers. The bullet holes in its wood are long patched, but the air inside still feels heavy.

Visitors today often report the sound of moaning drifting down the halls, or boots on the stairs when no one is there. Others claim to hear faint music — a fiddle, perhaps — rising from the tavern's lower rooms, as if the building itself remembers both the joy and the horror it has hosted. Paranormal enthusiasts insist that limestone beneath the tavern may amplify these phenomena, holding the emotional residue of the suffering like a recording.

One chilling tale tells of a tourist who entered the upstairs bedroom alone. She stood by the window when she suddenly felt pressure on her shoulder, as though someone had grasped her to steady themselves. Turning, she saw no one — but in the glass she glimpsed the reflection of a gaunt man in tattered gray, his face contorted in pain. The image vanished before she could scream.

Pope's Tavern remains a centerpiece of Florence ghost lore, its reputation built on the fact that so much death and fear once passed through its doors.

Wesleyan Hall

Wesleyan Hall, now part of the University of North Alabama, is a Gothic Revival building with turrets and towers that rise like something from a medieval battlement. Built in 1855 as a Methodist college, its romantic design belied the grim work it would soon perform. During the Civil War, Union troops occupied Florence repeatedly, and Wesleyan became both headquarters and barracks. The halls rang with the tramp of soldiers, the clatter of sabers, and the shouts of orders.

It is said that General William Tecumseh Sherman himself spent nights here, plotting campaigns by lamplight. The weight of decisions that would burn Georgia and break the South pressed into these walls. The building later returned to education, but the echoes of war never quite left.

Students and faculty whisper of figures in uniform roaming the halls after dark. Lights flicker in the towers where no one climbs. The sound of marching boots sometimes carries through the corridors at night, as though a ghostly regiment still drills in preparation for battle. Some report shadows darting across the stairwells or the sudden smell of tobacco smoke — sharp, acrid, unmistakable — though smoking has long been banned inside.

Paranormal theorists point again to Florence's limestone foundation. They suggest that the stone beneath Wesleyan Hall acts as a vast "battery," storing the residual energies of thousands of soldiers who once filled its corridors. Whatever the explanation, students alone at night often find themselves quickening their steps, glancing behind, certain they are being followed by boots that do not exist.

Soldiers' Rest – Florence City Cemetery

South of downtown lies Florence City Cemetery, where an area known as Soldiers' Rest was set aside for the Confederate dead. After the battles of Shiloh, Corinth, and Decatur, and after countless skirmishes across northern Alabama, bodies were brought here. Hundreds of soldiers were buried in neat ranks beneath simple markers, many of them unknown. Mothers came searching for sons. Widows wept at unmarked graves. The cemetery became a congregation of sorrow.

Today, Soldiers' Rest is quiet, but only on the surface. Visitors often describe hearing faint sobbing among the rows, or feeling sudden chills even on summer days. Some claim to see shadowy figures standing at the edge of the plots, watching silently before fading away. One local legend speaks of a spectral guard — a soldier in tattered gray who patrols the cemetery at night, musket on shoulder, as if still standing sentry over his fallen comrades.

The cemetery lies near limestone bluffs, and paranormal investigators suggest that the porous stone beneath helps "hold" the grief of the dead, magnifying the hauntings. Whether or not one accepts that explanation, few deny that the cemetery feels different after dusk. The air grows heavier, as though the weight of the war still presses down.

Mountain Tom Clark and the Booger Gang

Not all the spirits of north Alabama wear uniforms. In the late 1800s, long after the war, the region was terrorized by Thomas "Mountain Tom" Clark and his Booger Gang, outlaws who robbed, murdered, and left their victims in caves and woods. Clark bragged that "no one will ever run over Tom Clark." When he was finally captured and hanged in Florence in 1872, his body was left dangling for the crowd to jeer.

Clark's ghost, they say, did not rest. He is rumored to haunt the banks of Cypress Creek and the roads near Florence. Travelers speak of hearing harsh laughter in the night, or the pounding of hooves on dirt roads where no horse passes. Some claim to see a figure looming on a ridge, tall and broad, his eyes glinting before vanishing into shadow.

The connection between Clark's story and the Civil War is more than chronological. The chaos of war and Reconstruction created spaces where violence flourished. Outlaws like Clark thrived in the cracks left by battle. His ghost lingers as a reminder that the war's aftermath bred its own horrors, ones that walk the line between bandit and specter.

The Limestone Underworld

Beneath all these stories runs the limestone underworld — caves like Dust Cave, with its archaeological depths, or Red Bone Cave, whispered of in legends. Locals say these dark places connect in hidden ways, carrying sound and spirit alike. Paranormal researchers insist that limestone caves act as conduits, amplifying hauntings above.

In Lauderdale, Colbert, and Limestone Counties, caves are part of the landscape's skeleton. Farmers plowing fields have uncovered sinkholes that breathe cold air, as if the land itself were exhaling. Hunters exploring ridges stumble on mouths that swallow their lantern light. Many of these caves hold bones — some ancient, some from less distant tragedies. More than one explorer has emerged pale and shaken, claiming they heard whispers underground, voices echoing from nowhere, or the faint roll of drums deep in the stone.

It is tempting to dismiss such claims, yet the pattern persists. Where the limestone lies, the hauntings follow. Florence, with its mansions, taverns, halls, and cemeteries, stands atop a lattice of hidden caverns. Perhaps it is coincidence. Or perhaps the earth itself remembers.

Florence and Its Shadows

Today, Florence markets itself as a city of history and music — the home of W.C. Handy, the "Father of the Blues," and the site of thriving arts. Yet beneath the notes and murals, the ghosts remain. Sweetwater, Pope's Tavern, Wesleyan Hall, Soldiers' Rest — each is a chapter in a longer story, a story of blood spilled and sorrow unhealed.

The limestone caves underfoot only deepen the mystery. They are black arteries running beneath the city, unseen but always present, like the grief that lingers after war. Stand in Soldiers' Rest at twilight and you may hear a sob carried by the wind. Walk the halls of Sweetwater and you may feel a hand brush your shoulder. Step into Pope's Tavern and you may smell the iron tang of blood.

Florence is a city where history and haunting share the same rooms, where the war's echoes still move in shadows, and where the very ground seems to hum with memory.

The Haunted Confederacy has many capitals, but in Florence, Alabama, the dead have found their voice — carried in limestone, echoed in halls, whispered through caves that run forever beneath the earth.

Chapter 5 – Decatur: Ghosts of the River City

The Tennessee River curves like a silver blade through northern Alabama, wide and merciless, cutting deep into the land it nourishes. On its southern bank sits Decatur, a place that has always been defined by the river's moods. In the nineteenth century, the town grew as a crossroads of water and rail. Cotton bales rolled into warehouses, steamboats churned past its wharves, and locomotives shrieked across its tracks. Decatur was a hub of commerce, bustling with promise. But crossroads are never safe in wartime.

During the Civil War, Decatur became one of the most bitterly contested spots in Alabama. It was not a large town, but its geography was destiny. The river made it a gateway, and the railroads made it a lifeline. Both Union and Confederate forces knew they must hold it, and both were willing to bleed for it. That meant the little River City endured repeated occupations, skirmishes, and finally, in 1864, a siege that reduced it to rubble.

The people who lived through it never forgot. They told their children of nights spent in basements, of roofs collapsing in fire, of screams that carried down the river long after the guns were silent. And those who have come since say the memories never left. Shadows still move through the Old State Bank. Soldiers still tramp along Bank Street. The river still groans in the fog. Decatur rebuilt itself from ashes, but the ashes whisper still.

A Town Besieged

The first shots came early. In 1862, Union forces briefly occupied Decatur, recognizing its value as a railroad hub. Confederates countered, driving them out, only for the Union to return with more men. This tug-of-war went on for years, but it reached its climax in October 1864. Hood's Confederate Army, retreating after the disaster at Franklin, tried to force a crossing here. The Union garrison, outnumbered but entrenched, refused to yield.

For four days, the town shook with fire. Confederate skirmishers darted through its streets; Union sharpshooters fired from windows. Homes became fortresses, gardens trenches. Shells slammed into rooftops, setting fires that lit the night sky. One witness later recalled, "The town was like a furnace. Every house shook as though giants walked the earth."

When the smoke cleared, Decatur was a skeleton. Union accounts noted only four antebellum buildings still standing. Chimneys rose like gravestones, the rest reduced to ash. Families emerged from cellars and caves along the bluffs to find their lives obliterated. Women wept in the streets. Children clutched broken toys, their homes gone. The river carried away charred boards and, some whispered, bodies swept downstream.

This annihilation burned a scar into Decatur that still aches. It also laid the groundwork for the town's reputation as one of Alabama's most haunted places.

The Old State Bank

The Old State Bank is the grandest survivor of that fiery baptism. Built in 1833, its Greek Revival facade boasts five massive columns, weathered but defiant. Before the war it was a place of commerce, where ledgers balanced and coins clinked into drawers. During the war, it became something else entirely.

Union forces seized the bank and turned it into a hospital. The thick stone walls, meant to hold wealth, instead reverberated with screams. The vaults that once secured silver secured the wounded instead, their groans echoing like prayers in a crypt. Surgeons worked with saws and knives on makeshift tables, amputating limbs that piled outside in grotesque stacks. The marble steps, cool and elegant, were slick with blood carried down by orderlies.

Today, the bank is a museum by day — but by night, it is something stranger. Staff have reported cold drafts sweeping through sealed rooms. Tourists have glimpsed pale faces at the upstairs windows after closing. One janitor told of locking up only to hear dragging footsteps on the floor above. Convinced someone was left inside, he climbed the stairs. The hall was empty, but the footsteps continued, circling him, until they stopped behind his back. He turned and saw nothing, only the pale plaster walls and the darkness yawning deeper than it should.

Investigators speak of groans recorded on tape, moans that grow louder the closer one walks to the vaults. Some claim that if you press your ear to the stone at night, you will hear muffled prayers, as if the walls themselves are repeating the last words spoken within them.

The Dancy-Polk House

The Dancy-Polk House, built in 1829, is one of the oldest homes in Decatur. Its Federal-style design, with tall chimneys and a symmetrical facade, marked it as the residence of prominence. During the war, Union officers commandeered it as headquarters. Maps were spread across parlors, orders barked down stairwells, and cigars burned into the air. Locals crept past and muttered that the house was cursed now, its fine rooms poisoned by war.

The Dancy-Polk survived the firestorm that consumed the town, but not without absorbing its own shadows. Guests speak of the smell of cigar smoke lingering in the upstairs rooms, acrid and choking. Others describe hearing heavy boots climbing the staircase, only for the steps to fall silent halfway up. A woman touring the home once swore she felt a hand press against her sleeve as she descended, as though a harried officer were still rushing to his war council.

Caretakers have reported doors opening on their own, or the sound of furniture dragging across the floor in locked rooms. One chilling tale tells of a visitor who saw a group of men seated around a table in the parlor, their uniforms indistinct but their heads bent over maps. She blinked, and they were gone, leaving only the table, bare and dusted, and her own breath loud in her ears.

Shadows on Bank Street

Bank Street itself has a reputation. Once the commercial heart of Decatur, its warehouses and shops were gutted during the war. Today, restored brick facades give it charm, but after dark the street has an older feel. Residents walking home report hearing the tramp of soldiers in formation, boots slamming in unison on the pavement. Some hear the jangle of harness chains, or the low murmur of voices in cadence, as if an invisible column is marching through.

One man in the 1980s claimed to see an entire troop of soldiers materialize under the lamplight. He stood frozen as they passed — blue coats, rifles, their faces pale and expressionless. They turned a corner and vanished into mist. The man never walked Bank Street at night again.

Ghosts on the River

The Tennessee River was lifeblood and battlefield alike. Its waters carried steamboats and supplies, but they also carried war. Soldiers drowned attempting to cross under fire. Bodies floated downstream, their faces turned to the sky. Locals whispered that the river itself had become a grave.

To this day, the river bears stories. Fishermen report hearing musket fire crackling across the water on still mornings. Families walking the riverbank at dusk have seen figures in gray trudging toward the water, vanishing into fog as if marching into another world.

One chilling account from the 1970s tells of a family who saw soldiers walk onto the river as though it were solid. Their boots rang faintly on the surface before the fog swallowed them whole. Paranormal enthusiasts note the limestone bluffs and caves beneath Decatur, speculating that the stone amplifies these hauntings, carrying voices through fissures like whispers in a cathedral.

Even today, on misty dawns, the river groans with an otherworldly sound, as if the water itself remembers.

Decatur City Cemetery

When the battles ended, Decatur's dead were laid to rest in the city cemetery. Union soldiers were buried in neat rows, many without names. Confederate bodies were interred separately, often marked only with crude stones. The cemetery became a landscape of grief, each marker a story unfinished.

Visitors speak of a spectral guard who paces among the graves at night, musket on shoulder, vanishing if approached. Others claim to see a woman in black weeping at a grave that has no name, her sobs breaking the silence until they stop all at once. Caretakers have heard whispered prayers drifting among the stones at dusk, too soft to distinguish yet too real to ignore.

On Memorial Day weekends, tourists have reported seeing a soldier in blue standing at attention among the ranks, his form flickering like candlelight. One child once pointed at a grave and asked her parents why the "sad man" was crying there. No one else saw him.

The River City Today

Modern Decatur is a city of festivals, bridges, and industry. The hum of machinery and the laughter of crowds fill its streets. Yet beneath the new life, the old shadows remain. The Old State Bank looms with its haunted silence. The Dancy-Polk House whispers with footsteps from a vanished garrison. The cemetery lies heavy with unspoken prayers. And the Tennessee flows on, broad and indifferent, carrying whispers in its fog.

The River City is rebuilt, but it is never free. War burned itself into its bricks and into its water. At night, when the mist thickens and the lamps flicker, Decatur is not only a city of the living. It is a garrison of ghosts, their ranks unbroken, their march unending, their memories bound to the stone and river that made the town what it is.

Chapter 6 – Nashville: Phantom Camps and Haunted Hospitals

The Cumberland River slides broad and restless through Nashville, its surface catching the lamplight of a modern city that seems forever awake. Neon burns down Broadway, fiddles wail in every honky-tonk, and the sidewalks thrum with boots and laughter. But if you walk away from the noise, up into the hills or down toward the riverbank in the mist, the city changes. The shadows lengthen, the air thickens, and you can almost hear another Nashville layered beneath the living one — a Nashville of drums, of screams, of footsteps that will not cease.

This is the Nashville of the Civil War. A Union stronghold in the heart of the Confederacy. A hospital city where parlors became surgical theaters, churches rang with moans, and warehouses overflowed with the dying. A fortress city ringed with earthworks, its capitol bristling with cannon, its hills scarred by entrenchments. And finally, in December 1864, a battlefield where one of the war's last great Confederate armies was shattered in snow and smoke.

The dead of Nashville were many, and the stories of their restless spirits have never left. Today the city wears its scars in silence, but those who look closely can still see the imprint of war. Soldiers still march its hills. Hospitals still echo with cries. The Capitol still has a guard who never left his post. And when the winter nights grow long, whole phantom camps rise again in firelight that flickers and fades.

A City Under the Blue Flag

When Union troops captured Nashville in February 1862, the city changed overnight. It was one of the first Confederate capitals to fall, and the loss shocked the South. For the Union, it was a prize beyond measure: a hub of railroads, a river port, a city large enough to house armies and storehouses alike. Almost immediately, Nashville was swarmed with blue uniforms. Soldiers bivouacked on lawns, wagons rattled down streets, and the once-proud Southern capital became a garrison town.

Mansions were seized. Belmont, the estate of Adelicia Acklen — one of the wealthiest women in America — filled with troops. Churches that once rang with hymns became barracks or hospitals, their pews shoved aside for cots. Warehouses stuffed with cotton became commissaries stacked high with crates of bread, salt pork, and munitions.

The skyline itself became militarized. On St. Cloud Hill, enslaved men and impressed laborers built Fort Negley, the largest inland stone fort of the entire war. Its bastions loomed over the city, bristling with cannon. Hundreds of workers died quarrying the limestone, dragging blocks into place, laboring day and night under armed guard. Today Fort Negley's jagged ruins still stand, the grass grown thick over blood-soaked stone. Visitors often report shadows moving along the walls after dusk, or the sound of hammers echoing faintly though no one is there. Paranormal investigators call it one of the most haunted sites in Nashville, haunted not only by soldiers but by the spirits of the men who built it and never left.

The Battle of Nashville

Two years later, in December 1864, the city itself became a battlefield. Confederate General John Bell Hood, leading the remnants of his battered Army of Tennessee, marched north in desperation. His hope was to reclaim Nashville, to break Union hold on Tennessee. But Union General George H. Thomas was waiting, his forces dug in behind a network of fortifications.

The morning of December 15 dawned gray and bitterly cold. Civilians huddled in basements and attics, peering out windows at the armies spread across the hills. They could hear drums rattling, bugles crying, the tramp of thousands of boots. Then the Union line surged forward. Blue-coated troops stormed the Confederate redoubts, seizing cannon, driving the defenders from ridge to ridge. Snow and mud churned underfoot; the air filled with smoke so thick the sun vanished.

On December 16, Union forces struck again. At Shy's Hill, Confederate soldiers tried to hold their ground against overwhelming numbers. The hillside was steep, slippery with frost and blood. Witnesses said men slid down the slopes, bayonets flashing, muskets cracking in deafening waves. By nightfall, Hood's army was broken. Survivors fled south in chaos, leaving thousands of dead and wounded behind. One Union officer later wrote, "It was as if the earth itself groaned. The fields were pale not with snow, but with faces turned upward in death."

Those fields are neighborhoods now — houses, lawns, gardens. But residents swear that on cold December nights, the hills remember. Phantom musket fire crackles in the darkness. Shapes move among the trees, flickering in and out of sight. The cries of the dying drift through the air, carried on winter winds. Shy's Hill, Peach Orchard Hill, Montgomery Hill — all are said to harbor restless dead who cannot forget their last stand.

Haunted Hospitals of Nashville

The Union made Nashville into a city of hospitals. By 1864, nearly every large building was converted into one. Schools, churches, and mansions overflowed with the wounded. Even the fairgrounds were turned into sprawling medical camps.

St. Mary's Orphanage and Hospital. During the war, Catholic nuns tended the dying here, washing wounds and whispering prayers. Many soldiers breathed their last in those halls. Later staff claimed to hear the rustle of skirts when no one was present, or the soft murmur of prayers in empty rooms. Patients swore they saw nuns gliding through corridors only to vanish. Some called them angels; others said they were shades who had never left their charges.

Belmont Mansion. Adelicia Acklen's opulent estate became Union headquarters. Soldiers tramped across its marble floors; officers slept in velvet-draped bedrooms. Legends say some of the wounded were treated in its halls. Visitors today report footsteps on the grand staircase, whispers in the parlors, and the sudden sound of a piano playing though the room is empty. Guests on tours sometimes glimpse a Union officer on the lawn, his coat buttoned high against the cold, vanishing before their eyes.

Two Rivers Mansion. Built just before the war, this Greek Revival home was occupied by troops. Locals say dying men were carried inside, their blood staining the floors. Today, lights flicker in its windows, doors slam of their own accord, and a spectral figure in uniform has been seen pacing the veranda, as if still on guard duty.

Union General Hospital No. 8. This vast hospital treated thousands. Its walls absorbed screams, saws, and sobs. Long after it was demolished, people walking near its former grounds reported hearing groans, or the rattle of gurneys moving over stone.

Nashville was a city of healing and death at once, and its hospitals remain some of its most haunted sites.

The Capitol and Its Phantom Guard

The Tennessee State Capitol dominates the city from its limestone hill. Designed in Greek Revival style, it was already a symbol of authority before the war. During the Union occupation, it became fortress and headquarters. Cannon bristled from its slopes; Union soldiers drilled on its lawns. Andrew Johnson, appointed military governor of Tennessee, worked inside, trying to hold a divided state together.

Guards patrolled its corridors night and day. Some of them, it seems, still do. Visitors after hours have reported hearing footsteps echoing on marble floors when the building is empty. Others describe the shadow of a man pacing in the rotunda, musket in hand, who vanishes when approached. Staff have heard the faint notes of a bugle drifting through the halls, mournful and lingering, though no musician stood there.

Legend holds that one particular guard, who died on duty, still refuses to abandon his post. Late at night, a cold wind sometimes sweeps the staircases, and those who walk alone say they feel eyes on them — steady, watchful, unblinking.

Camps of Ghosts

In 1864, the hills around Nashville blazed with Union campfires. Soldiers filled every ridge, their songs, laughter, and curses carrying through the valley. Locals remembered the sight of endless white tents, the glow of thousands of fires like stars fallen to earth.

After the war, some said those camps never left. On cold December nights, flickering lights have been reported on the slopes of Shy's Hill and other battlegrounds. From a distance, they look like campfires, arranged in neat rows. But when approached, they vanish.

Hikers have stumbled onto groups of shadowy men seated as if around a fire, only for the figures to dissolve into mist. Others describe the sound of drums rolling through the dark, or the thin, reedy call of fifes. Sometimes the music swells into a full martial band, only to fade before the source can be found.

One family walking at dusk swore they saw a line of soldiers trudging across a field, their rifles on shoulders, their heads bowed. The family stood aside to let them pass — but the column simply melted into the night, leaving only silence.

Prisons of Sorrow

Nashville was also home to prison camps, where captured Confederates endured harsh conditions. Some were confined in old warehouses, others in makeshift stockades. Disease, hunger, and exposure killed many. Their shallow graves lined the outskirts of the city.

Residents later told of moans drifting through the air near these sites, of rattling chains echoing in the night. Travelers described gaunt figures moving along the roads, faces pale, eyes hollow, before vanishing into shadows. One former stockade site, it is said, still produces cries on winter evenings, as if the ground itself remembers.

Cemeteries of the Fallen

Nashville National Cemetery, just northeast of the city, holds over 33,000 Union dead. The rows of white stones stretch to the horizon, a sea of sacrifice. Visitors speak of a spectral sentry who marches among the graves, musket at his shoulder, vanishing if approached. Others claim to see ghostly processions — long lines of soldiers moving silently between the rows, their heads bowed.

Confederate dead lie in other cemeteries across the city. In some, mourners claim to hear weeping in the dusk, or see lanterns bobbing among the graves as if grieving families from long ago are still searching for their loved ones. One woman walking through Mount Olivet Cemetery swore she saw a lady in black kneeling at a grave. When she approached, the figure vanished, leaving only the faint scent of roses.

Nashville Today

The Nashville of today is alive with music. Broadway glitters with neon; the Ryman echoes with song. But beneath the honky-tonks and skyscrapers lies a haunted city.

Walk the grounds of Belmont at night, and you may hear piano notes drifting through empty halls. Stand before the Capitol at dusk, and you may feel the chill of a watchful guard. Climb the slopes of Shy's Hill in December, and you may see fires that vanish when you approach, or hear the roll of drums that never stop.

Nashville is a city of light, but it is also a city of shadows. Its stages are built on battlefields; its streets run over graves. The phantom camps and haunted hospitals remind us that war does not end when the guns fall silent. In Nashville, the war is still marching, still moaning, still waiting in the mist.

Chapter 7 – Mississippi's Haunted Vicksburg and Corinth

The air above the Mississippi River is heavy, thick with humidity even at twilight, and the river's broad sweep bends like a serpent at the foot of Vicksburg's bluffs. The city rises high above the water, its brick streets climbing steep hills, its ridges crowned with old oaks that have seen war and ruin. To stand here at dusk is to feel the weight of history pressing close — the muffled boom of cannon fire that once shook the earth, the cries of thousands starving in darkness, the groans of the wounded in churches turned into morgues.

Mississippi's Civil War story is, in many ways, the story of Vicksburg and Corinth — two strongholds that became synonymous with struggle, blood, and loss. At Vicksburg, a city starved and bombarded into submission by Union forces, the bluffs themselves became honeycombed with caves where desperate families hid from fire raining from the sky. At Corinth, the railroads that defined the Confederacy's lifeline turned the town into a crossroads of battle, where the ground trembled with clashes so fierce that locals swore they could still hear the echoes long after.

The ghosts of these places are not pale footnotes. They are vivid, restless, and unforgettable. Walk the trenches of Vicksburg or the crossroads of Corinth, and you may hear the phantom rumble of drums, the clash of bayonets, or the faint sobbing of children who never escaped the caves.

These cities are more than memorials — they are haunted landscapes where the war never truly ended.

Vicksburg: The City That Would Not Surrender

In 1863, Union General Ulysses S. Grant set his eyes on Vicksburg. The Mississippi River was the key to victory, and Vicksburg — perched on high bluffs overlooking a sharp bend — was the lock. Confederate President Jefferson Davis himself called it "the nailhead that holds the South's two halves together." As long as Vicksburg stood, the Confederacy had hope of uniting east and west across the river.

From May 18 to July 4, Grant's army encircled the city. Cannon roared day and night, shells screaming overhead to burst in fire and iron. Trenches crept closer each week, cutting into the red clay, until Union lines nearly strangled Vicksburg. Inside, life turned to nightmare.

Food dwindled. Rats fetched high prices. Mules were slaughtered, their meat boiled into stringy stews. Shoes and belts were boiled for broth. A Confederate diarist wrote, "We are eating everything but the earth itself." Civilians dug caves into the hillsides, turning the bluffs into a warren of burrows. Families huddled underground while artillery shook the ground above. By candlelight, mothers tried to hush their children's cries as dust fell from the ceilings with each explosion.

It is said the caves themselves are haunted. More than one collapsed, entombing entire families alive. Paranormal investigators describe these places as "psychic echo chambers," their limestone walls storing trauma like grooves in a record. Explorers who venture near report whispers in the dark, or the sound of a child crying softly where no child lives. One man swore he felt a tug on his sleeve deep inside a cave, though he was alone.

When surrender finally came on July 4, Vicksburg was gaunt, hollow-eyed, and broken. But the ghosts had only begun to stir.

Haunted Bluffs and the Shirley House

Today, the Vicksburg National Military Park preserves the battlefield, its hills rolling and green, monuments standing tall. But as the sun sets, the land shifts. Visitors speak of sudden chills, the air heavy with something unseen. At the Railroad Redoubt, where Union troops stormed the Confederate defenses in one of the siege's bloodiest assaults, tourists have reported the clash of muskets and the screams of dying men erupting without warning, only to fade into silence. One visitor fainted on the spot, later insisting she had felt the ground shake under her feet as though hundreds of men were charging past.

The Shirley House is the lone surviving wartime home inside the park, its white frame weathered but still standing. Union troops occupied it, using it as a hospital. At night, rangers have seen lights flickering in the windows though the building is dark. Curtains twitch without wind. Guests whisper of faces peering out at them — gaunt, hollow-eyed soldiers watching from the shadows of a house that refuses to be empty. Some even claim to hear piano music drifting faintly from inside, a tune played by hands long gone.

Soldiers' Rest and the Lantern Lights

Cedar Hill Cemetery holds a section called Soldiers' Rest, where thousands of Confederate dead lie. Some markers bear names; many are "Unknown." By day, it is a solemn, peaceful place. But by night, shadows move.

Caretakers tell of lanterns bobbing among the rows, as though mourners still search for loved ones. One described seeing a line of gray-coated figures walking silently between the stones, their heads bowed. Another swore a soldier saluted him before dissolving into mist. Visitors often leave shaken, not by fear but by sorrow, as if the dead are still trying to be seen.

Local legend insists that on July 4, the anniversary of surrender, the cemetery becomes most active. Voices chant prayers in the dusk, bugle notes drift faintly through the air, and phantom processions march in silence, remembering a day that broke the Confederacy's back.

Corinth: The Crossroads of Blood

Two hundred miles east, in Corinth, Mississippi, the war carved its own scars. The town was small, but its railroads made it invaluable. The Memphis & Charleston line ran east to west; the Mobile & Ohio ran north to south. Together they formed a crossroads Confederates could not afford to lose.

After the carnage of Shiloh in April 1862, Confederate forces withdrew to Corinth. Grant's army besieged the town, capturing it in May. That summer, disease ran rampant in the swampy camps, killing more soldiers than bullets. Then in October, Confederate General Earl Van Dorn tried to retake Corinth. His men hurled themselves at Union earthworks in two days of savage fighting. The attacks collapsed, leaving streets littered with bodies.

Locals said the ground itself seemed cursed. Blood soaked into clay so deeply that grass would not grow in certain patches for years. The cries of the dying carried down alleys and into parlors turned into hospitals. To this day, residents claim Corinth has never fully rid itself of the stench of smoke and death.

The Contraband Camp and the Songs That Linger

Corinth became a refuge for formerly enslaved men and women who flocked to Union lines. The Union established the Corinth Contraband Camp, housing thousands. Life was hard, and many died of disease and deprivation, but it was also a place of first freedom.

Visitors today report hearing singing on the site — faint voices rising in spirituals. Some say the songs are mournful, others hopeful, as though the spirits are still reaching toward freedom. One ranger described hearing "Swing Low, Sweet Chariot" drifting across the fields at night, though no one was near. He said the voices were layered, like a choir, and when he walked toward them, they faded into silence.

Haunted Depots and Mansions

The old railroad depot, now the Crossroads Museum, is alive with echoes. Staff have heard the roar of phantom trains, whistles shrieking as though locomotives thunder past though the tracks are empty. One volunteer late at night heard men shouting orders in the depot, their voices urgent. She searched the building room by room. It was empty.

The Verandah House, an antebellum mansion, served as Confederate General Braxton Bragg's headquarters. Tourists speak of cold spots in its halls, or the sense of being watched. Some claim to see Confederate officers standing on the staircase, faces stern, eyes hollow. One woman fainted after seeing a man in gray looking straight at her before dissolving into air.

Churches and hotels pressed into service as hospitals are said to groan with residual energy. At the site of the Tishomingo Hotel, where countless wounded were treated, passersby report phantom cries and the slam of doors though no building remains. On some nights, locals swear they hear the rumble of ambulance wagons along the old streets, their wheels creaking in the dark.

The Phantom Battle

Perhaps Corinth's most chilling legend is the phantom battle. Residents say that on quiet nights, especially in October, the clash returns. Musket fire rattles in the dark, cannon roar, men scream. Sometimes the noise is faint, like distant thunder. Other times it erupts so vividly that listeners are certain armies are fighting in the fields again.

One farmer recounted seeing whole regiments appear in a field near the earthworks — lines of men surging forward, bayonets gleaming, smoke rolling over them. He froze, too terrified to move. Then, as quickly as they appeared, the soldiers melted into mist, leaving only silence. The farmer never doubted his eyes.

Mississippi's Haunted Ground

Mississippi's Civil War story is written in blood, stone, and ghostlight. At Vicksburg, the caves whisper with the voices of starving children, and the bluffs echo with the thunder of phantom cannon. At Corinth, phantom trains roar, soldiers clash in fields, and spirituals rise from the Contraband Camp as if sung by voices that refuse to be silenced.

Walk the trenches of Vicksburg at dusk, and you may feel cold fingers brush your arm. Stand in Soldiers' Rest at midnight, and you may see lanterns bobbing through the fog. Visit Corinth's crossroads, and you may hear orders shouted, drums rolling, battle crashing. Mississippi holds its dead close, refusing to let them go.

The war here was more than history. It was a tearing of the land itself — and the land has never healed. The ghosts of Mississippi are reminders of wounds too deep for time to close, lingering in every bluff, every rail, every cave where the living once trembled and the dying cried out.

Chapter 8 – Georgia's Haunted Kennesaw and Andersonville

Georgia is a land of red clay and rolling ridges, a place where the soil seems to hold memory as tightly as it holds the roots of its oaks and pines. During the Civil War, the land here became both battlefield and grave, its hills and fields carved by trenches, its towns filled with the moans of the dying. Two names stand out above all others in Georgia's haunted landscape: Kennesaw Mountain and Andersonville.

Kennesaw Mountain was the site of one of Sherman's bloodiest defeats — a brutal, futile charge against fortified Confederate lines in June 1864. The mountain became a slaughterhouse where thousands of men fell in the space of a few hours. To this day, hikers speak of phantom gunfire, the Rebel yell echoing through the trees, and lines of ghostly soldiers trudging eternally uphill.

Andersonville, officially Camp Sumter, was worse than any battlefield. It was a prison designed for ten thousand that swelled to more than thirty thousand, where starvation, disease, and exposure consumed nearly thirteen thousand Union men. Visitors today describe the weight of despair pressing into their bones, phantom cries for water, and lantern lights drifting through the National Cemetery.

In both places, the veil between past and present seems worn thin, as if the land itself refuses to let go of the horrors it absorbed.

Kennesaw Mountain: Sherman's Bloody Slope

By the summer of 1864, General William T. Sherman was driving deep into Georgia on his march toward Atlanta. Confederate General Joseph E. Johnston chose Kennesaw Mountain, a towering ridge northwest of the city, as his fortress. His men dug trenches along the rocky slopes, positioning cannon and sharpshooters in a seven-mile line bristling with death.

Sherman had maneuvered Johnston backward for months, outflanking him again and again. But at Kennesaw, Sherman lost patience. On June 27, he ordered a frontal assault. Union soldiers advanced across open ground beneath a blazing sun, their bayonets flashing, their uniforms already soaked in sweat. Confederate cannon roared from the heights, tearing holes in the advancing lines. Muskets rattled from trenches above. Men fell by the hundreds.

A Union officer recalled, "We advanced as if into the jaws of hell itself. The air grew hot with lead. Men were dropping all around me, some without a cry, others screaming for their mothers."

By the time the attack faltered, nearly three thousand Union soldiers were dead or wounded. The Confederate lines stood, their earthworks piled with the bodies of attackers. Sherman admitted defeat, one of the few times he did so in the war.

The Dead Angle at Cheatham Hill

The bloodiest point of all was Cheatham Hill, where Union troops hurled themselves at a Confederate angle so narrow and so fierce that bodies piled into walls. Survivors used the dead as cover, propping rifles against corpses to fire. The ground was soaked, and the cries of the wounded went on for hours.

Today, Cheatham Hill is called "the Dead Angle," and those who walk it say the name is not metaphorical. Visitors describe sudden pressure on their chests, as if the air itself thickens. Some cannot breathe, forced to leave the site in panic. Others hear moaning just beyond the trees, or voices whispering "Forward!" on the wind.

One hiker reported seeing dozens of shadowy forms sprawled across the ground as dusk fell, their outlines pale against the earth. He blinked, and they were gone. Paranormal investigators have recorded disembodied voices: cries of pain, the command "Fire!", the sound of men groaning. Skeptics scoff, but those who have walked Cheatham Hill after dark rarely laugh.

Echoes on the Mountain

Kennesaw Mountain itself seems to breathe. Rangers tell of footsteps crunching leaves behind them, but when they turn, the trail is empty. On foggy mornings, hikers glimpse entire regiments trudging uphill — men in tattered uniforms, muskets on shoulders, their faces gray and indistinct.

Campers near the base hear the roll of drums at night, joined by the high, thin notes of fifes. One woman awoke to find her tent surrounded by men in gray, their eyes hollow. She screamed, and the figures vanished like smoke.

Some believe the land itself amplifies these hauntings. Georgia's ridges are shot through with quartz and limestone, minerals that paranormal theorists say can "record" trauma like a phonograph. If that theory holds, Kennesaw Mountain is one of the largest recordings of horror in the South — a place that replays its agony endlessly.

Andersonville: The Prison of Shadows

If Kennesaw was a slaughterhouse of battle, Andersonville was a slaughterhouse of neglect. Officially Camp Sumter, the Confederate prison opened in February 1864. It was designed for ten thousand

Union prisoners of war. Within months, it held more than thirty thousand.

The stockade was twenty-six acres enclosed by fifteen-foot pine logs. Inside, there were no shelters, no barracks — only open ground. Prisoners dug holes in the earth to escape the sun, covering them with scraps of cloth. The single water source, a small creek running through the camp, was quickly polluted by human waste.

Disease ran rampant. Dysentery, scurvy, typhoid — men wasted away, their bodies gaunt, their gums bleeding. Food was meager, often rotting cornmeal. Starvation carved hollow eyes into faces. Men killed rats for meat.

By the time the camp closed, nearly thirteen thousand Union soldiers were dead. Their bodies were buried in trenches, row upon row. Andersonville became a name synonymous with horror, its commandant, Captain Henry Wirz, hanged for war crimes after the war.

The Weight of Despair

Visitors to Andersonville National Historic Site often describe a sensation unlike anywhere else. The moment they step onto the prison ground, the air grows heavy. Some say they feel crushed, as though grief itself presses into their bones. Rangers tell of tourists bursting into tears without knowing why.

Paranormal investigators speak of cold spots even in summer heat, batteries draining instantly, and moans captured on recorders. Many claim to hear cries of "Water!" in the stillness — the desperate plea of men who died of thirst. Others describe rattling chains, or the shuffle of countless footsteps in mud.

One chilling tale tells of a visitor walking alone at dusk. He saw a ragged figure in blue trudging across the field, his uniform in tatters, his face hollow. The man raised a hand as if to beg for help. When the visitor rushed forward, the figure vanished, leaving only silence and the overwhelming stench of decay — a smell no one else detected.

Providence Spring

In the midst of suffering, one miracle came. In August 1864, after months of thirst, a thunderstorm struck Andersonville. Rainwater carved a new spring through the stockade wall, bubbling fresh water into the camp. Prisoners hailed it as divine intervention, naming it Providence Spring.

The spring still flows today, crystal clear. But it, too, is haunted. Visitors filling bottles report feeling hands brushing theirs, unseen but insistent. Some hear murmured prayers of thanks near the water, voices layered as if a crowd is gathered, though the field is empty. Others see gaunt men kneeling at the spring, scooping water into their hands before vanishing like mist.

Andersonville National Cemetery

Just beyond the prison lies Andersonville National Cemetery, where the dead rest in endless rows. White markers stretch across green fields, many carved only with "Unknown." It is a place of sorrow so deep it seems carved into the air.

Caretakers tell of seeing lantern lights moving among the graves at night. Some hear weeping, low and mournful, rising from nowhere. Others speak of whispered prayers drifting through the grass, voices impossible to understand yet undeniably human.

One visitor swore she saw a procession of soldiers marching silently between the stones, their heads bowed. They moved in perfect formation before fading into nothing. Another told of a man in tattered blue standing at attention near the gate, saluting her before dissolving into mist.

Georgia's Haunted Ground

Georgia holds both battle and prison in its haunted soil. On Kennesaw Mountain, the thunder of phantom artillery rolls across ridges, soldiers forever climbing a slope they cannot conquer. At Andersonville, the cries of the starving echo on hot winds, and lanterns drift among the graves of the unknown.

Stand on Cheatham Hill at dusk, and you may feel bodies pressing against you, the weight of men falling all around. Walk the prison ground at Andersonville, and you may hear the endless plea for water, the shuffle of thousands of invisible feet.

The war carved Georgia into a landscape of pain, and the land has never forgotten. The Haunted Confederacy finds some of its darkest chapters here — not just battles fought in blood, but suffering endured in silence. These places are more than memorials. They are living echoes, proof that the past has claws.

Savannah: The Haunted Port

Savannah's cobblestone streets and moss-draped oaks make it one of the South's most beautiful cities, but its beauty is laced with shadow. During the Civil War, Savannah was spared the torch when Sherman's army marched in December 1864, the city surrendered rather than face destruction. But even without fire, Savannah was a city of occupation, anxiety, and mourning.

Many of its grand houses became hospitals, where soldiers lingered between life and death. The Sorrel-Weed House, famous even before the war, became notorious after. Visitors today report soldiers in gray moving across its halls, their boots echoing on wooden floors long after midnight. Disembodied voices have been recorded, whispering orders or cries of pain.

At Madison Square, where Confederate hospitals once overflowed with the wounded, people have seen apparitions of gaunt men limping across the grass. One woman described watching a figure stagger, clutching his side, before he collapsed and vanished into the earth. Guides on ghost tours often note how many guests suddenly feel faint or short of breath on this spot, as though their bodies briefly relive the pain of the dying.

Savannah's riverfront, too, is said to be haunted. The cotton warehouses that lined the wharves became makeshift barracks for Union troops after the surrender. Sailors walking the waterfront at night have reported phantom music drifting from empty buildings, and others have seen shadowy men in uniform staring out over the water, their faces lined with sorrow.

Milledgeville: The Confederate Capital of Georgia

While Savannah was spared destruction, Milledgeville — Georgia's capital during the war — was not. In November 1864, Sherman's men marched into the town. They held a mock legislative session in the Statehouse, symbolically repealing

Georgia's secession. They ransacked homes, tore up streets, and desecrated churches. For the proud town, it was humiliation etched into memory.

The Old Governor's Mansion, a grand Greek Revival home, had been the seat of Confederate governors. When Union troops took it, the house became both trophy and barracks. Visitors today swear its halls are restless. Doors slam when no one is near. Footsteps echo across empty rooms. Some claim to see a tall man in a frock coat — perhaps a governor who refuses to leave his home to the occupiers. Others hear the laughter of Union soldiers echoing faintly in the night, a mocking sound that chills the blood.

At Central State Hospital, originally the Georgia State Lunatic Asylum, the war years left scars as well. Confederate soldiers wounded in the Atlanta Campaign were housed there, many dying far from home. The hospital grew into one of the largest asylums in the world, with its own reputation for hauntings. Locals tell of figures wandering the grounds at dusk, indistinct and sorrowful. Some are said to be patients; others wear tattered uniforms of the 1860s.

A Haunting Legacy

Together, Savannah and Milledgeville widen the map of Georgia's ghostly Civil War. Savannah whispers with soldiers who surrendered their city but not their presence. Milledgeville echoes with governors, soldiers, and patients who never left the grand halls or hospital grounds.

Walk the oak-lined squares of Savannah at dusk, and you may hear boots on cobblestones, voices muttering in the fog. Stand in the Old Governor's Mansion at midnight, and you may feel eyes watching from the shadows. Georgia's Civil War was fought in its hills and prisons, but its ghosts still linger in its cities, reminding us that no place — no matter how beautiful — escaped the war's shadow.

Chapter 9 – Spiritualism and the Southern Dead

The Civil War ended with silence. The cannons ceased, the bugles quieted, and the clash of armies faded into memory. Yet across the South, silence was not peace. It was absence. Empty chairs stood at supper tables. Black crepe fluttered from doorways. Graveyards swelled with hurried burials, while countless others lay unmarked in fields far from home. The dead were everywhere, yet unreachable.

In that vacuum, a strange hunger grew. Families longed not just to remember their dead but to hear them again, to know they had not vanished into nothingness. Spiritualism — a movement already stirring in America before the war — surged into prominence, transforming grief into ritual, hope into ceremony. In parlors lit by flickering lamps, widows and mothers gathered around tables, listening for knocks, whispers, and shadows. For them, ghosts were not legends. They were family.

The South, shattered by war and humiliation, became fertile soil for this desperate faith. Its cities and towns, lined with battle-scarred homes and hospitals reeking of death, seemed haunted already. Spiritualism did not create ghosts in the South — it simply gave them a stage.

The Rise of Spiritualism Before the War

The first whispers of spiritualism came not from Dixie but from the North, with the Fox Sisters of Hydesville, New York. In 1848, these young girls claimed to communicate with a ghost through coded raps. Their story captured the American imagination. Within a decade, séances had become fashionable from Boston to Baltimore. Tables rocked, trumpets floated, and mediums claimed to channel the voices of the dead.

Before the Civil War, the South regarded spiritualism with mixed suspicion and curiosity. Ministers condemned it from pulpits as heresy, while some society ladies indulged in it as a parlor amusement. But when war came, and the dead multiplied by the hundreds of thousands, curiosity turned to desperation.

A Region in Mourning

Imagine the South in 1863. In nearly every town, there are houses draped in black. Women wear mourning veils that stretch to the ground, some refusing to remove them for years. Courthouses nail lists of the dead to their doors, names read aloud to hushed crowds. In churchyards, coffins are lowered one after another, until the earth itself seems swollen with sorrow.

In this atmosphere, the living turned to any hope of bridging the chasm. Families gathered not just in churches but in candlelit parlors. Children sat wide-eyed at tables where their mothers prayed for a sign from fathers killed at Shiloh, Chickamauga, or Franklin. The war had turned half the South into orphans and widows. Spiritualism promised that loss did not mean separation.

The Southern Séance

Picture a parlor in Savannah, its shutters drawn tight. A widow sits at the head of a polished mahogany table, flanked by neighbors in black. A medium — perhaps a traveling woman from the North, perhaps a local with sudden reputation — lays her hands on the table's edge. The candles flicker though no breeze stirs. Then comes the sound — three sharp raps under the floorboards.

Gasps ripple through the room. The widow clutches her breast. "Is that you, Thomas?" she whispers. Another knock. The medium's eyes roll back. She speaks in a strange voice, deeper than her own: "I am here."

For those present, the moment is not theater. It is deliverance. Whether fraud or miracle, it does not matter. The widow leaves that night believing she has spoken with her husband. Her grief has been given shape, her silence filled with presence.

Stories of such séances abound. In Montgomery, Alabama, a circle of women swore that a table lifted from the floor and spun before dropping with a crash. In Nashville, a medium claimed to see rows of Confederate soldiers standing at attention behind their mothers, their faces pale and stern. In Macon, a séance ended when the parlor piano struck three notes though no one touched the keys.

Ghosts in the Churches

The South's churches became battlegrounds not only for war but for the soul. Many had been stripped of pews to serve as hospitals. Blood stained their floors, and the dying moaned where hymns had once rung. After the war, when congregations returned, some found their sanctuaries changed.

Worshippers in Tennessee told of shadowy figures kneeling at altars where soldiers had once lain. In Georgia, mourners claimed to hear weeping during sermons, only to find no one behind them. Ministers thundered against spiritualism, denouncing mediums as agents of Satan. Yet their own churches whispered with the presence of the dead, undermining every condemnation.

In rural camp meetings, where revival tents filled with fervor, the supernatural mingled with the sacred. People fainted, not from the preacher's fire but from unseen hands brushing their shoulders. Some swore the shouts of hallelujah were answered by voices not of the living.

The Mourning South

Mourning in the South became nearly a profession. Etiquette guides outlined proper dress and behavior for widows, who might wear black for years. Some households left chairs empty at dinner tables, or places set for sons never returning.

Spiritualism fit seamlessly into this culture of mourning. To seek contact with the dead was not frivolous; it was an extension of duty. Widows in Atlanta flocked to mediums who promised even a word from the beyond. Mothers clung to scraps of paper said to bear their sons' spectral handwriting.

In Mobile, a woman claimed to dream of her husband every night until a medium told her to hold a séance. When she did, she said his spirit appeared and told her he was at rest. After that, the dreams ceased.

Folklore and the Phantom South

Spiritualism in the South did not remain confined to parlors. It bled into folklore, joining older traditions of ghost tales. Stories of spectral soldiers began to circulate — gray-clad men seen on moonlit roads, headless horsemen galloping past farmhouses, women in black weeping at cemetery gates.

One famous story from Alabama tells of a woman wandering Decatur's cemetery, crying for her son. Witnesses said she vanished when approached, leaving only the sound of sobbing. Locals began to whisper of "the Weeping Mother," blending mourning custom with ghostly presence.

Such tales blurred the line between séance and superstition. For Southerners, ghosts were not abstractions. They were the neighbors, the sons, the husbands lost to war.

Andersonville and the Séance of the Dead

Nowhere did spiritualism find more fertile ground than at Andersonville. Survivors spoke of the prison's horrors for decades, their stories feeding nightmares. In the late 1800s, a group of widows visited the site with a medium. They sat near Providence Spring, calling upon the dead.

One woman claimed she saw hundreds of gaunt figures rise from the earth, their hollow eyes fixed upon her. Another fainted, saying she heard her husband call her name. The medium screamed that the ground itself was alive with spirits. Those who witnessed it swore never to return, but the tale spread like wildfire.

Andersonville was a wound that could never close. Spiritualism gave it voice, making the cries of the prisoners eternal.

The South's Haunted Legacy

By the turn of the twentieth century, spiritualism had been exposed in many quarters as trickery. The Fox Sisters confessed their fraud. Famous mediums were caught using wires and hidden assistants. Yet in the South, the belief never fully died.

Because the war's wounds were so deep, the stories endured. Grandmothers whispered to grandchildren of séances where they spoke to fathers lost in gray. Families handed down tales of pianos playing by themselves, of phantom knocks on parlor tables, of soldiers standing watch at night.

Ghost stories became part of Southern identity, woven into the fabric of memory. They were not just entertainment. They were a way of keeping the dead close.

Closing the Circle

Picture, once more, a Southern parlor at twilight. The shutters are drawn, the candles lit. Around the table sit mothers and daughters, their hands clasped tight. A knock sounds underfoot. The medium speaks: "Who is here?" A whisper answers, faint but certain.

For the mourners, that whisper is salvation. They leave believing they have touched eternity, if only for a moment. And perhaps they have.

For the South, haunted by war, spiritualism was more than a fad. It was survival. It was a bridge across absence. It was the only way to endure a world where ghosts outnumbered the living.

Even now, when the South tells its ghost stories, it is not simply recounting folklore. It is continuing a conversation begun in those darkened parlors — a conversation with the Southern dead, whose voices still echo in the silence left by war.

Chapter 10 – Alabama's Shadowed Roads: Mountain Tom Clark and the Booger Gang

The Civil War cast a long shadow over North Alabama. Its armies passed back and forth across the Tennessee River, leaving farms burned, towns scarred, and cemeteries overflowing. But in the cracks left behind, in the lawless spaces between Union occupation and Confederate defense, another shadow grew. It was not an army, nor even deserters taking refuge in the hills. It was a gang — rough men without loyalty, who preyed upon their neighbors in the chaos of war.

At their head stood Mountain Tom Clark. His name alone conjured dread. His companions were known as the Booger Gang, a title whispered to frighten children into staying close to home after dusk. They robbed, murdered, and terrorized across Lauderdale, Colbert, and Limestone Counties. They left behind not just crimes but a curse — and a legacy of hauntings that locals still whisper about on dark nights.

The Making of a Villain

Little is known of Clark's early years, but folklore fills the gaps. Some say he came from the high ridges of Tennessee, hardened by hunger and violence. Others claimed he had "the devil in his eyes" even as a boy. By the time war came, Clark had no allegiance to North or South. He thrived in chaos.

To the people of Florence and Tuscumbia, Clark was a man without conscience. Tall and broad, with a booming voice, he carried himself with the swagger of one who believed no law could touch him. Those who crossed him described his glare as cold and reptilian, a look that made grown men falter.

The Booger Gang

Clark did not work alone. Around him gathered a band of ruffians who came to be called the Booger Gang. Their name came from a mixture of fear and folklore. To rural families, a "booger" was a monster or spirit used to frighten children. The gang leaned into the name, appearing at night masked or smeared with soot, their laughter carrying across dark fields.

They robbed stagecoaches along the Memphis-to-Charleston line, ambushed ferries on the Tennessee River, and stormed into isolated farmhouses. Survivors of these encounters spoke of boots kicking in doors, of lantern light flashing on pistols, of families herded into corners as valuables were stripped away.

The gang's crimes were not limited to theft. Murders mounted. Farmers vanished after refusing to hand over livestock. Freedmen were found beaten in the woods. Soldiers home on furlough disappeared on the road between Florence and Athens. The Booger Gang became less a gang of men and more a nightmare that walked the night.

The Wilson Plantation and the Death of a Preacher

Among the many stories tied to the Booger Gang, none has echoed louder than the death of Rev. Charles B. Handy, father of William Christopher Handy — the man who would one day be called the Father of the Blues.

Local legend holds that the gang attacked the Wilson Plantation, where Rev. Handy was employed. Accounts differ, but the folklore insists that Clark's men killed the preacher in cold blood, leaving his family bereft. While historians debate the exact truth — some records suggest Handy died of other causes — the community long believed the outlaws responsible.

To many, the haunting tones of W.C. Handy's later music carried that grief. The blues, born of sorrow and struggle, seemed to contain in their mournful strains the echo of a father lost violently. Locals whispered that the Booger Gang's cruelty had helped shape America's music — their evil transformed into art through the mourning of a son.

At the Wilson Plantation itself, stories abound of restless spirits. Workers and visitors claim to see lanterns bobbing in the fields at night, or hear gunshots on still evenings. Some say the shadow of a man in a preacher's coat can be seen walking the grounds, his head bowed, vanishing when approached. Paranormal investigators have reported phantom knocks inside the old quarters and voices whispering in recordings — unintelligible, but undeniably human.

The Capture and the Curse

By 1872, Florence had had enough. Citizens banded together to capture Mountain Tom Clark, finally overwhelming him and dragging him to face justice. His trial was swift. There was no shortage of witnesses to his crimes, and the entire county demanded retribution.

When the gallows were built, crowds filled the square. Women, children, soldiers — all gathered to see the outlaw hang. Clark, however, did not beg. As the noose was placed around his neck, he looked out at the crowd and laughed.

"Florence!" he shouted. "You'll never forget me! I'll haunt this place till the end of time!"

His words rang across the square. Moments later, the trap gave way, and his body swung. But those who witnessed it said his curse lingered, echoing in their ears long after the crowd dispersed.

Hauntings of the Outlaw

The stories began almost at once. Some said Clark's body bled when touched, refusing to rest. Others swore that at night his ghost walked the streets, rope still dangling from his neck, his laugh echoing in the dark.

Travelers along the roads Clark once prowled reported phantom riders galloping past, their horses pounding though the road was empty. Farmers told of hearing coarse laughter outside their windows at midnight, though no one stood there.

Children grew up with the warning: "Don't stray too far after dark — the Booger Gang will get you." Parents spoke the words to scare them straight, but the tremor in their voices suggested belief.

Phantom Riders and Lantern Lights

The Tennessee River, broad and dark beneath the bluffs of Florence, carries its own stories. Fishermen swore they saw riders on horseback racing across the water, their hooves striking sparks before vanishing in spray. Others told of a phantom ferry, drifting silently with shadowy figures aboard — outlaws damned to wander forever.

Near the Wilson Plantation, lanterns have been seen weaving through the trees, their glow bobbing in the dark. Locals say these are the Booger Gang, cursed to forever search for victims they can never reach. In some stories, the lights vanish suddenly, leaving behind the sound of distant gunfire or the echo of mocking laughter.

Haunting the Courthouse and Gallows

The site of Clark's execution also carries whispers. Florence's courthouse square has been the scene of footsteps pacing after dark, the sound of heavy boots grinding into gravel though the square is empty. Guards once posted there swore they heard choking gasps on the wind, as though the gallows had been raised again.

Some claim to see a tall man in shadow standing near the old site, his form indistinct, but a rope clearly around his neck. A local policeman, patrolling near midnight, reported seeing such a figure. When he approached, it melted into mist, leaving behind only the acrid smell of smoke.

Modern Echoes

Paranormal investigators who have come to Florence often focus on Mountain Tom's legacy. Some bring recorders into cemeteries, capturing laughter on playback — rough, sharp, and cruel. Others use thermal cameras along the roads, claiming to catch flickering figures on horseback, too tall and indistinct to be human.

Ghost tours in Florence still tell the story of Clark's curse, their guides lowering their voices as they describe his last words. Visitors often leave uneasy, swearing they feel eyes watching them as they walk back to their cars.

Even descendants of the Handy family speak of strange occurrences at the old plantation — sudden gunfire on a clear night, or shadows moving across windows when no one is inside. Some believe Rev. Handy's restless spirit still lingers, tethered to the injustice of his death.

Outlaws Among Soldiers

What makes Mountain Tom's haunting distinct among the South's ghostly tales is its nature. Soldiers haunt out of sorrow, duty, and unfinished business. Outlaws haunt out of defiance. Clark's ghost is no mourning sentinel; it is a predator's shadow, a menace that refuses to fade.

The South is filled with spectral soldiers — men marching, bugles sounding, lanterns bobbing among graves. But Clark is remembered as a figure of terror, his spirit carrying the same malice he showed in life. His haunting is not one of sadness but of threat, a reminder that war breeds not only heroes but monsters.

Closing Reflection

The shadowed roads of North Alabama remain haunted, not just by armies but by men like Mountain Tom Clark. His curse lingers in Florence, in lanterns that flicker on empty roads, in laughter that cuts through the dark, in the phantom riders said to thunder across the river.

To walk those roads at night is to risk hearing them yourself — the echo of hooves, the glint of a lantern, the sharp bark of a laugh. And in that moment, the words Clark spat from the gallows ring true once more: Florence will never forget him.

Because Mountain Tom Clark, outlaw and murderer, keeps his promise. His ghost still walks Alabama's shadowed roads.

Chapter 11 – Conclusion: The Haunted Confederacy

The war has long been over, yet the South still breathes its memory. Cannon fire no longer shakes the valleys, and no regiments march across the fields with muskets in hand, but something remains. It is not only carved into monuments or etched into marble headstones. It lingers in the air, in the soil, in the very bones of the land. The South is a place where history has not gone silent but continues to whisper, echo, and sometimes cry out in the dark.

To write of the Civil War in the South is to write of a haunted region. The haunted houses, the battlefields, the prisons, and even the outlaw roads are not isolated curiosities. Together, they form a second history — one told not through official records but through flickering lanterns, phantom bugles, and shadows that refuse to fade. This is the Haunted Confederacy, where the past will not release its grip, where the living and the dead still walk side by side.

The Land of Ghosts

Stand at Shiloh's Bloody Pond at dusk, and the water seems to ripple though the air is still, as if disturbed by bodies no longer there. Walk through the cedar glades at Stones River, and you may hear the faint echo of drums, the bugle calling troops who never answered. At Chickamauga, Green Eyes still prowls the hills, part animal, part spirit, part grief made flesh.

Move south into Franklin, and the Carter House still breathes sorrow. The Lotz House whispers with children's laughter cut short, while Carnton's floors remain stained with blood that will not wash away. The weeping soldier stands eternal at the cemetery, stone tears echoing the real tears of widows who walked those grounds.

In Florence, Alabama, Sweet Water and Pope's Tavern hold footsteps that no broom can sweep away. Wesleyan Hall echoes with cadets' boots. Soldiers' Rest glows with phantom lanterns. Beneath the ridges, limestone caves twist and turn — stone vaults that paranormal researchers say record tragedy like grooves in a record. And in those same hills, Mountain Tom Clark curses still, his Booger Gang galloping down dark roads, lanterns weaving through fields, laughter sharp as broken glass.

Decatur, with its old bank and riverside battle scars, still smolders with spectral gunfire. Nashville, proud and scarred, is haunted by phantom camps and soldiers' processions through Mt. Olivet. Vicksburg remembers in caves where whispers of trapped families linger, while Corinth resounds with phantom trains and choirs of voices rising from the Contraband Camp.

Georgia groans under the weight of Kennesaw and Andersonville. At Cheatham Hill, breath becomes hard, as though the air thickens with bodies falling again and again. Andersonville cries with thirst, moaning voices begging for water, while Providence Spring flows as both miracle and haunting. Savannah's moss-hung streets cradle soldiers who still stagger across Madison Square, and Milledgeville's Governor's Mansion stands with footsteps pacing its halls, defiant governors and mocking occupiers tangled together forever.

This is the haunted geography of the Confederacy. Each place is a chapter of grief. Together, they are a chorus of the dead.

The Human Cost That Would Not Fade

The Civil War killed more Americans than any other conflict. The toll was beyond counting in some communities, where every household lost a son or father. The South, with its fields turned to battlefields and towns turned to ashes, bore the deepest wound. In such a place, sorrow could not simply end. It pressed down, generation after generation, until it became folklore, ritual, haunting.

Ghosts here are not only specters. They are embodiments of grief too heavy to bear in silence. A woman weeping at a grave in 1865 becomes a story told in 1885, a warning whispered in 1925, and a ghost tour stop in 2025. The dead linger because the living could not forget them, and in remembering, they gave them voice.

Spiritualism and the Aftermath

When black crepe draped the South's doors, when mourning dresses dragged in the dust for years, families turned to any hope of hearing the voices of their dead. Spiritualism rose like wildfire, séances lit by candles, tables tilting, knocks sounding in the night. For some, it was a parlor trick. For the South, it was survival.

A mother in Montgomery begging a medium for one last word from her son. A widow in Nashville clutching a table as a trumpet's hollow voice whispered her husband's name.

A family in Savannah, certain the piano played by unseen hands as their lost child returned for a moment.

Spiritualism in the South was not curiosity — it was desperation. It blended with the land's own folklore until ghost stories became as common as hymns. Churches thundered against séances, yet their own sanctuaries groaned with the spirits of soldiers who had died upon their floors.

The South learned to live with its ghosts. To this day, it still does.

Outlaws and Soldiers

The South's haunted memory is not reserved for soldiers alone. Men like Mountain Tom Clark remind us that war breeds predators as well as martyrs. Clark's curse on Florence and the phantom riders of the Booger Gang are as much a part of Alabama's lore as Shiloh's phantom drums. His haunting is different: not sorrowful but malicious, a reminder that cruelty leaves its own shadow.

Together, these tales reveal the full spectrum of haunting: noble soldiers saluting at their graves, starving prisoners crying for water, children's voices laughing in ruined homes, and outlaws mocking from the dark. Each reflects a piece of the war's legacy — sacrifice, suffering, loss, and terror.

The Haunted Confederacy Today

The South has embraced its ghosts. From Savannah's ghost tours to Nashville's battlefield reenactments, from Florence's outlaw stories to Andersonville's solemn memorials, the region lives with its haunted past. Paranormal investigators bring recorders and thermal cameras, capturing voices that mutter from the air. Tourists walk battlefields by lantern light, their guides whispering of phantom regiments and haunted mansions. Descendants still tell family stories of séances, knocks, and dreams that seemed too vivid to dismiss.

This living relationship with the dead is unique. The South does not hide its hauntings. It builds them into its identity, its storytelling, even its economy. Yet beneath the entertainment, the grief is real. Every lantern-lit tale is also a reminder of chairs that sat empty, of sons buried far from home, of women who walked veiled in black for decades.

One Last Walk

Picture this: it is twilight on a Southern battlefield. The cicadas hum, the air is heavy with the smell of pine and dust. You walk alone, but you do not feel alone. The fields are wide and silent, yet a pressure settles on your chest.

From the tree line comes a faint sound — the rattle of drums, a bugle calling troops long dead. Shadows flicker, men in blue and gray trudging across the field. A figure pauses, looks at you with hollow eyes, then fades into mist.

You keep walking, the grass brushing your legs. A lantern glimmers ahead, swaying as if carried by an unseen hand. You follow, though the field is empty. The light winks out, leaving only the deepening night. Yet the air feels alive, humming with memory.

This is the Haunted Confederacy. A place where the past does not sleep, where the dead walk with the living, and where history itself has claws.

Final Reflection

The Civil War tore the South apart, and the land has never let it go. Its ghosts are not relics of fear but reminders of sacrifice, suffering, and sorrow. They march still, they cry still, they haunt still — because the war is not finished in memory.

To step into the South is to step into a living ghost story. It is to walk among echoes of the past, to feel their eyes on you, to hear their voices when the night is still. The Haunted Confederacy endures, not because the living keep telling the stories, but because the dead refuse to stop telling them.

And so the South remains a place unlike any other — a place where history whispers in the dark, where lanterns glow with no hand to hold them, and where ghosts walk forever, reminding us that war never truly ends.

Printed in Dunstable, United Kingdom